JUDAIZING JESUS

JUDAIZING JESUS

HOW NEW TESTAMENT SCHOLARS
CREATED THE ECUMENICAL GOLEM

ROBERT M. PRICE

Pitchstone Publishing
Durham, North Carolina

Pitchstone Publishing
Durham, North Carolina
www.pitchstonebooks.com

Library of Congress Cataloging-in-Publication Data

Names: Price, Robert M., 1954- author.
Title: Judaizing Jesus : how New Testament scholars created the Ecumenical
   Golem / Robert M. Price.
Description: Durham, North Carolina : Pitchstone Publishing, [2021] |
   Includes bibliographical references. | Summary: "Questions the scholarly
   consensus that Jesus was a mainstream or sectarian Jew and offers a new
   theory of Christian origins by proposing alternative ways of seeing
   Jesus"— Provided by publisher.
Identifiers: LCCN 2021028183 (print) | LCCN 2021028184 (ebook) | ISBN
   9781634312134 (paperback) | ISBN 9781634312141 (ebook)
Subjects: LCSH: Jesus Christ—Jewishness. | Jesus Christ.
Classification: LCC BT590.J8 P75 2021 (print) | LCC BT590.J8 (ebook) |
   DDC 232.9/06—dc23
LC record available at https://lccn.loc.gov/2021028183
LC ebook record available at https://lccn.loc.gov/2021028184

CONTENTS

INTRODUCTION

Recently something of a scholarly consensus has emerged that Jesus must have been a mainstream (or perhaps some identifiable sort of sectarian) Jew, and that we must automatically adopt Second Temple Judaism as the paradigm in which to interpret or reconstruct the historical Jesus. This consensus view is often presented as self-evident and unquestionable, a priori and apodictic. This raises serious questions whether the promotion of the Jewish Jesus is actually the product of theological and ecumenical agendas. Things continue as they have since at least 1997 when J. Duncan M. Derrett wrote:

> A struggle goes on between those who, since the 1940's, have been discarding anti-Semitism and searching for Jesus amongst the debris of Judaic thought, and those whose future hangs upon a predetermined approach to their hero, blocking discoveries which encourage a realistic investigation of the available materials.[1]

The situation presupposes the state of Historical Jesus studies where both the blessing and the bane are an embarrassment of riches; there are so many gospel data pointing in so many directions and susceptible of many, diametrically different, interpretations. There

---

1. J. Duncan M. Derrett, *Some Telltale Words in the New Testament* (Shipston-on-Stour, Warwickshire: Peter Drinkwater, 1997), p. 1.

is a perhaps unavoidable circularity in that one begins by tentatively imposing an interpretive paradigm onto the data (e.g., "What if Jesus were an apocalyptic prophet? A revolutionary messiah? A community organizer? A feminist? A Galilean hasid?"). Then one uses that hunch as a yardstick against which to measure the gospel material. What is compatible with one's hypothesis becomes central, everything else peripheral, secondary, inauthentic embellishment. As the discussions of Postmodernism suggest, every paradigm comes with its own criteria of plausibility, effectively sealing it off from alternative paradigms.

Thomas Kuhn[2] reflected that in the end there may be no objective basis for one's choice among competing paradigms, and that one's preference is something like a religious conversion. I suggest that Kuhn put his finger on what is going on in the choice of the Jewish Jesus model (and of course many others). Theological agendas make this option more attractive to many scholars.

And yet it remains possible to weigh the alternatives with something like objective criteria that Kuhn himself set forth. We ought to prefer any paradigm that makes the most sense of the data without resorting to ad hoc hypotheses ("epicycles"); a model that interprets the data in the most natural and inductive manner given the historical-cultural setting; a paradigm that has "predictive" value in providing a way to make sense of new questions and to unlock hitherto "anomalous data" in the sources.

Using these criteria, I will evaluate the exegetical-evidential basis for today's "Jewish Jesus" models (there are more than one), analyzing the cases made by Geza Vermes, James H. Charlesworth, Richard A. Horsley, Bruce Chilton, Hyam Maccoby, Daniel Boyarin, and others, Christian and Jewish, conservative and liberal, asking what theological and ecumenical agendas motivate each tendency. Then I will ask after the possible alternatives for a historical Jesus if we find

2. Thomas S. Kuhn, *The Structure of Scientific Revolutions* (Chicago: University of Chicago Press, 1962), pp. 150,156–157.

we must dismiss the popular "Jesus within Judaism" reconstructions.

My hypothesis is that the widespread position that Jesus must be assumed to have been essentially a devout practitioner of Second Temple Judaism is the product of ecumenical and apologetical agendas and does not survive close, genuinely critical scrutiny. The peeling away of most of the textual evidence for a Jewish Jesus may leave us with an unsatisfying agnosticism. If we may take apocalyptic to stand for Judaism in general, we are faced once again with Albert Schweitzer's dilemma: either thoroughgoing eschatology or thoroughgoing skepticism, and we may have to choose the alternative he rejected.

I will argue that many attempts to elucidate the meaning of various gospel texts by supplying "implicit" Jewish background data are better understood as (unwitting) attempts to pull texts innocent of such concerns into a Judaizing framework. I will argue that certain key gospel passages that make Jesus speak the language of traditional Judaism are historically inauthentic and so should not contribute to a reconstruction of the historical Jesus. I suspect, then, that much of the "Jewish Jesus" or "Rabbi Jesus" industry is manufacturing an ecumenically viable Jesus, an interfaith bargaining chip. This is likely the hidden (?) agenda of theologically liberal scholars. But there is an equally strong tendency for scholars to interpret the historical Jesus as far as possible in conventional Jewish categories in order to ward off theories of theologically distasteful influences on Christianity from Hellenistic Mystery Religions and Gnosticism. To admit influence from these quarters would undermine the notion that New Testament doctrine, especially Christology, is the direct product of supernatural revelation. "Gnosticism and Mithraism have not revealed it unto thee, but my Father in heaven." I detect this urgency in critics like Raymond E. Brown as well as apologists like Edwin Yamauchi and William Lane Craig. Here again, "Jewishness" is code for "Old Testament," from which Christianity must be the true-born child.

PART ONE
THE ECUMENICAL GOLEM

٦ PRINCE OF PEACE TREATY

Michael B. McGarry[3] comments on the statement "Israel: People, Land, State" issued by the National Catholic-Protestant Theological Dialogue in 1973, which "explicitly repudiates any Christology which would understand that the Jewish covenant has been invalidated since Christ's coming. In this sense the Christology operative here seems to be a negative one; that is, whatever Christians believe about Christ cannot mean that the Jews have been abandoned by God, nor has God ceased to bless Jewish worship as an abiding expression and place of his blessing." The document is not a piece of New Testament scholarship or, really, scholarship of any kind. It is a nominally theological *policy statement*. Thus it is merely a paper compromise ("You say this and we'll say that, okay?"). That is problematic enough, but it seems to me that the same is ultimately true in the case of the "Jewish Jesus" models we are about to consider. See if you don't think I'm right.

Now here's one from the other side of the bargaining table. Shaul Magid[4] opines that "The continuing project of Jewish Americaniza-

3. Michael B. McGarry, *Christology After Auschwitz* (New York: Paulist Press, 1977), p. 59.

4. Shaul Magid, "The New Jewish Reclamation of Jesus in Late Twentieth-Century America: Realigning and Rethinking Jesus the Jew," in Zev Garber, ed., *The Jewish Jesus: Revelation, Reflection, Reclamation* (West Lafayette: Purdue University Press, 2011), p. 359.

tion (also called Jewish identity) requires a new Jewish Jesus that can address the changing nature of Jesus in American Christianities." Magid[5] certainly views a proposal of Irving Greenberg (to be considered later) in this light: "For Greenberg, Jesus is a tool of ecumenism, a means to cultivate a new relationship between Judaism and Christianity in a post-Holocaust world. He is not trying to reclaim Jesus as much as complicate the very notion of the messiah in order to meet his Christian interlocutors half way." Bingo!

Eva Marie Fleischner proposed to retitle Jesus as the non-offensively ecumenical "Jesus, Son of Abraham." "It is scriptural, yet not worn thin through use; it points to Jesus' 'Jewishness' through his descent from Abraham, father of the Jewish people; it is not a Messianic title, such as 'Son of David,' hence acceptable to Jews."[6] For Monika Hellwig, following Edward Schillebeeckx, "Jesus is the place of encounter of man with the transcendent God, which Christians have experienced as central in all human existence."[7] I think here of a college motto in a cartoon I once saw: "Standing for nothing, offending no one."

"A healthy appropriation of the Jewish Jesus will avoid the kind of reverential tones that one sometimes hears from Jews who want to emphasize interreligious dialogue so much that they talk of Jesus as a prophet and teacher in order to show Christians that now we can be nice to him" (Michael Lerner).[8]

---

5. Magid, p. 366.

6. Eva Marie Fleischner, *Judaism in German Christian Theology Since 1945: Christianity and Judaism Considered in Terms of Mission.* ATLA Monograph # 8 (Metuchen, NJ: Scarecrow Press, 1975), p. 125, quoted in McGarry, p. 76.

7. Quoted in McGarry, p. 95. I was privileged to have both Fleischner and Hellwig as teachers, the first at Montclair State College, the second at Princeton Theological Seminary. I also heard Schillebeeckx speak once but could not understand a single sentence. (I had better luck with his books.)

8 Michael Lerner, "Fresh Eyes: Current Jewish Renewal Could See Jesus as One Like Themselves." In Beatrice Bruteau, ed., *Jesus Through Jewish Eyes: Rabbis and Scholars Engage an Ancient Brother in a New Conversa-*

James Charlesworth tells us: "Neither [group of critical scholars, both Christian and Jewish] began moving in this direction [i.e., understanding Jesus as a faithful Jew] in order to improve the relations among Jews and Christians. The conclusion is not dictated by such contemporary concerns. The perspective, which is now a presupposition [!], underlying much research on first-century times, does, however, become the foundation for bridge building among contemporary Jews and Christians."[9] I'm afraid I don't buy it. This is like William Lane Craig saying, fingers crossed behind his back, that he believes in Jesus' resurrection because the Holy Spirit tells him it's true but that, luckily, the evidence *happens* to supports the same conclusion!

You can see where all this is headed from the words of Bernard J. Lee:[10] "What ways of interpreting his Christological meaning are available to us that do not themselves step outside of Jesus' Jewishness?" What would be a good name for such an approach? Perhaps "Christmas List Christology" would do? Would not such a Jesus aptly be called an *ecumenical Golem*, artificially constructed, not by Rabbi Lowe[11] but this time by well-meaning Christian and Jewish theologians?

---

tion (Maryknoll: Orbis Books, 2001), p. 147.

9. James H. Charlesworth, "Jesus, Early Jewish Literature, and Archaeology," in Charlesworth, ed., *Jesus' Jewishness, Exploring the Place of Jesus in Early Judaism*. Shared Ground Among Jews and Christians: A Series of Explorations Volume II (New York: American Interfaith Institute/Crossroad, 1991), p. 197.

10. Bernard J. Lee, *The Galilean Jewishness of Jesus: Retrieving the Jewish Origins of Christianity*. Conversation on the Road not Taken –Volume 1. A Stimulus Book (New York: Paulist Press, 1988), p. 18.

11. Gustav Meyrink, *The Golem*. Trans. Hugo Steiner-Prag and Madge Pemberton (New York: Dover Publications, 1985).

ANOINTED ANTINOMIAN

We might pause a moment to remind ourselves of just what approach to Jesus these ecumenical diplomats are reacting against. Of course, there is the familiar Lutheran Jesus who aimed to bring Judaism (i.e., the Torah) to an end and to replace it with Christianity. This model has been important even to modern critical Protestants like Adolf Harnack and Ernst Käsemann. One ventures to suggest that Paul was more important to their perspective than Jesus. As most read Paul at the time, he believed that "Christ is the end of the Law for everyone who believes" (Rom. 10:4). Thus it was natural to understand Jesus as a good Paulinist who then must have negated the Torah. And this in spite of Matthew 5:17, which our Protestants took to mean Jesus brought the Torah to fulfillment by fulfilling its predictions of his own coming. Joachim Jeremias was a pious Lutheran and could not help reading Jesus as one. For Jeremias, Jesus' gospel tidings were that God was declaring amnesty for all who would believe in him. He could dine with sinners precisely because God had pardoned them.

Ethelbert Stauffer was perhaps the strongest advocate for a non- or anti-Torah Jesus:

> many of the sayings of Jesus recorded in the Gospels, which have hitherto been considered authentic because they sounded characteristic of Palestinian Judaism, are more likely to have derived from the doctrinal traditions of the era preceding Jesus (the theology of the group around John the Baptist) or the era succeeding Jesus (the teachings of the Palestinian Christians). These sayings were incorporated into the very oldest traditions concerning Jesus in the course of a major effort to re-Judaicize his message.[12]

> Matthew betrays the inveterate Jewish dislike of the Samaritans, who were regarded as no better, and in fact far worse, than

---

12. Ethelbert Stauffer, *Jesus and his Story*. Trans. Richard and Clara Winston (New York: Alfred A. Knopf), p. xi.

the pagans. This was a Jewish or Judao-Christian attitude, but it was not that of Jesus.[13]

It seems pretty obvious that Matthew imports scribal concerns into his gospel (Matt. 12:5; 13:51–52; 23:2, 8–10, 16–22; 24:20), adding such material to his Markan source and therefore can be said to Judaize (or to *re*-Judaize) the gospel tradition, but our question, and Stauffer's, is a larger one: has the Jesus character been overhauled in the direction of Judaism or Pharisaism? Stauffer's answer was clear:

> Matthew had a theological interest in the concept of the Messiah. This was an outgrowth of the tendency of his circle to re-Judaicize the message of Jesus. Consequently he inserted references to the messianic idea throughout his gospel, and at crucial points put the statement into Jesus' mouth. All this was a part of a campaign to rewrite history for dogmatic ends.[14]

As for the historical Jesus, he "was making his official break with the Torah."[15] As "long as he had been under the influence of John, he had remained unconditionally faithful to the Torah."[16] But "Now Jesus proclaimed new tidings of God, a new religion that in principle was no longer bound by the Torah."[17] In "his conflict with the Torah"[18] "he deliberately violated the law and invited others to do the same."[19] Stauffer's reading of Matthew 11:25–30 makes it sound positively Marcionite!

13. Stauffer, p. 71.
14. Stauffer, p. 161.
15. Stauffer, p. 73.
16. Stauffer, p. 75
17. Stauffer, p. 76.
18. Stauffer, p. 77.
19. Stauffer, p. 171.

At that time Jesus answered and said, "I thank you, Father, Lord of heaven and earth, that you have hidden these things from the wise and prudent and have revealed them to babes. Even so, Father, for so it seemed good in your sight. All things have been delivered to me by my Father, and no one knows the Son except the Father. Nor does anyone know the Father except the Son, and the one to whom the Son wills to reveal him. Come to me, all you who labor and are heavy laden, and I will give you rest. Take my yoke upon you and learn from me, for I am gentle and lowly in heart, and you will find rest for your souls. For my yoke is easy and my burden is light."

Stauffer comments:

the apostolic church did everything in its power to neutralize this 'scandalous' saying and the revolutionary aspect of Jesus which it expressed. The Jesus of the Synoptic Gospels does bring forth scriptural proofs and does practice exegesis of the Torah, again and again. But the words quoted in Matthew 11, 25 ff, tower above the layers of the Synoptic tradition like a lonely and primordial peak—the solid rock of the authentic Jesus.[20]

Darned if it *doesn't* sound Marcionite! This Jesus introduces a new God unknown to the human race, and he lifts from humanity's shoulders the splintery yoke of the Torah, as in Acts 15:10. And Stauffer echoes Marcion in blaming the apostles and their church for failing to grasp Jesus' truth. His Jesus was introducing "a new religion."

Stauffer, though technically not a card-carrying member of the Nazi Party, wrote *Our Faith and Our History: Towards a Meeting of the Cross and the Swastika* (1933). In 1957 he wrote, "The primary role of Jesus research is clear: De-Judaizing the Jesus tradition."[21] Yikes!

---

20. Stauffer, p. 169.

21. Ernst Klee, *Das Personenlexikon zum Dritten Reich* (2nd ed.: Frankfurt am Main: Fischer Taschenbuch Verlag, 2005), p. 598.

2 THE CIRCUMCISION PARTY

DISSING DISSIMILARITY

Charlesworth and his colleagues lament Norman Perrin's[22] attempt to isolate what was distinctive about Jesus rather than what Jesus and his contemporaries may have shared in common, because their agenda is to submerge Jesus into the Judaism of his day, minimizing his distinctiveness. To this end they seek to widen the net to make more of the gospel sayings "authentic." This endeavor also comports with their disdain for what Schweitzer called the "thoroughgoing skepticism"[23] approach. They want to "know" something quite specific about Jesus, namely that he was a Jewish rabbi. Sean Freyne is one such.

Instead of dissimilarity, with its tendency to provide a minimal-

---

22. "But if we are to seek that which is most characteristic of Jesus, it will be found not in the things that he shares with his contemporaries, but in the things wherein he differs from them." Norman Perrin, *Rediscovering the Teaching of Jesus* (New York: Harper & Row, 1976), p.39; Rudolf Bultmann, *The History of the Synoptic Tradition*. Trans. John Marsh (New York: Harper & Row, rev. ed. 1968), p. 205.

23. Albert Schweitzer: *The Quest of the Historical Jesus: A Critical Study of its Progress from Reimarus to Wrede*. Trans. W. Montgomery (New York: Macmillan, 1968), Chapter XIX, "Thoroughgoing Scepticism and Thoroughgoing Eschatology," pp. 330–397.

ist amount of tradition, [Gerd Theissen] now proposes a criterion of historical plausibility as the most suitable formulation to address the issue of the historical Jesus as currently debated. Plausibility is explained with reference to both influence and context, thereby broadening considerably what can in principle be judged as authentic within the Jesus tradition by giving priority to coherence over dissimilarity. His formulation of the criterion seeks . . . to locate Jesus firmly within the cultural milieu of his Jewish co-religionists (his context)—aspects of his history that the criterion of dissimilarity had by definition excluded. Theissen formulates his ideas about this latter aspect as follows: "Whereas the criterion of difference requires that it should not be possible to derive Jesus traditions from Judaism . . . the criterion of plausible historical context requires only a demonstration of positive connections between the Jesus tradition and the Jewish context, i.e. between Jesus and the land, the groups, the traditions and the mentalities of the Judaism of that time."[24]

Charlesworth again:

I am convinced that we find our way to the greatest historical certainty by excluding (at least in the beginning) those Jesus sayings that can be attributed to the needs and concerns of the earliest 'Christian' communities. But it seems unwise to tighten this criterion further by eliminating material that has its roots in Early Judaism. If a particular saying is discontinuous with the needs or motives of the earliest Christians, it does not necessarily render it inauthentic if it has points of contact with Early Judaism.[25]

---

24. Sean Freyne, *Jesus a Jewish Galilean: A New Reading of the Jesus-story* (London/New York: Trinity Press International, 2004), p. 12, quoting Gerd Theissen and Annette Merz, *The Historical Jesus: A Comprehensive Guide*. Trans. John Bowden (London: SCM Press, 1996), p. 117.

25. Charlesworth, *Jesus within Judaism*, p. 6.

And there are more: "Our increased understanding of its diversity has made it more difficult to be sure precisely what kind of Jew Jesus was and against which historical background we should try to understand him" (Daniel J. Harrington).[26] "At a few points we may catch glimpses of distinctive features, perhaps even a measure of originality. But our approach to the study of Jesus is not driven by a quest for uniqueness or originality" (Craig A. Evans).[27]

"[W]hat is Jewish in Jesus' teaching is not unique, and what is unique is not Jewish," says Andrew Vogel Ettin.[28]

"If our understanding of the historical Jesus is to be modeled on such familiar historical types, he does not bring anything to the universe of Jewish experience that would not be present without him" (Daniel F. Polish).[29]

But among this brotherhood of *haberim* we occasionally detect a note of—dissimilarity! Though a Jewish Jesus advocate, Morris Goldstein admits that "what is likely to be recorded [in the Jesus tradition] would be what is startling, dramatic, not customary."[30] Marcus J. Borg seems to be aware of the Achilles heel of the dissimilarity criterion as a means of identifying authentic Jesus sayings: "When dissimilarity does appear, one cannot be certain that the Jesus level

26. Daniel J. Harrington, "The Jewishness of Jesus: Facing Some Problems" in Charlesworth, ed., *Jesus' Jewishness*, p. 123. You mean Jesus is dissimilar to Judaism after all? Ironically, Harrington himself blasts the dissimilarity criterion on pp. 132–133.

27. Craig A. Evans, "The Misplaced Jesus: Interpreting Jesus in a Judaic Context." In Bruce Chilton, Craig A. Evans, and Jacob Neusner, *The Missing Jesus: Rabbinic Judaism and the New Testament* (Leiden: Brill Academic Publishers, 2002), p. 30.

28. Andrew Vogel Ettin, "That Troublesome Cousin." In Beatrice Bruteau, ed., *Jesus Through Jewish Eyes: Rabbis and Scholars Engage an Ancient Brother in a New Conversation* (Maryknoll: Orbis Books, 2001), p. 69.

29. Daniel F. Polish. "A Jewish Reflection on Images of Jesus." In *Jesus Through Jewish Eyes: Rabbis and Scholars Engage an Ancient Brother in a New Conversation* (Maryknoll: Orbis Books, 2001), p. 96.

30. Morris Goldstein, *Jesus in the Jewish Tradition* (New York: Macmillan, 1950), p. 102.

of the tradition has been reached, but only that a stage of tradition has been reached that is so opaque that the interests of the community are no longer known."[31] That is to say, there is no way to be sure some saying that cannot be readily seen to serve some early Christian faction does not after all stem from a forgotten segment of early Christianity unknown to us. But elsewhere Borg seems to have forgotten what he'd said. He now thinks we can rely on "primitive tradition elements which do not reflect known interests of early Christianity, 'which it is improbable that the Church in light of its theological development should ever have invented.'"[32]

PRESUPPOSITIONALISM

Is Jesus to be read as a teacher of the Torah? Should such an assertion be a conclusion, or rather a presupposition? Charlesworth is only too happy for the circularity: "Far too many New Testament scholars still fail to scrutinize the presupposition that the historical Jesus is unknowable and lost forever behind the creative editing of the evangelists. . . . These docetic acids eat away the earthly dimensions, including the Jewish beliefs of Jesus, and his earliest followers. . . . We must discard the presupposition that Jesus was not a Jew."[33] Of course, nobody's going *that* far,[34] not even Reichsführer Stauffer.

Daniel Boyarin is but one of the self-fulfilling prophets: "By now, almost everyone recognizes that the historical Jesus was a Jew who

---

31. Marcus J. Borg, *Conflict, Holiness and Politics in the Teaching of Jesus* (Harrisburg: Trinity Press International, 1998), p. 38.

32. Borg, p. 40, quoting W.D. Davies.

33. James H. Charlesworth, ed., *Jesus' Jewishness*, p. 15.

34. On the other hand, see Paul Haupt, *The Aryan Ancestry of Jesus* (*The Open Court* vol. XXIII, No. 4, April, 1909, no. 635; rpt. San Diego: Amory Stern, 2020); Richard Wagner, Houston Stewart Chamberlain, Paul Haupt, and A.C. Cuza, *Galilee Against Judea: Wagnerian Bible Criticism*, ed., Amory Stern (San Diego: Amory Stern, 2020); Jacob Elon Connor, *Christ Was not a Jew: An Epistle to the Gentiles* (CPA Book Publishers, 1936)..

followed ancient Jewish ways."[35] Likewise: "Layer after layer must be removed in order to penetrate to the original countenance of Jesus. But this countenance and this form do not stand in an empty space; they must be examined within the context of the Palestinian Judaism contemporary to him. Any other viewpoint fails to see the true nature of Jesus" (Schalom Ben-Chorin).[36] "[T]he new shape of the so-called quest for the historical Jesus . . . comes from taking very seriously the Jewishness of Jesus and trying to understand him within the limits of first-century Judaism."[37]

James H. Charlesworth: "Now, I am convinced that the new discoveries, *sensitivities*, [my emphasis] and methods compel us to strive to see Jesus within his contemporary Jewish environment. The thesis of this book is simple: Jesus of Nazareth as a historical man must be seen *within* Judaism."[38]

Bruce Chilton: "Because discussion over the past fifty years or so has greatly enhanced the critical appreciation of Judaism, it is sometimes assumed that what is understood of Judaism can be transferred directly to the assessment of Jesus."[39] All too true, even though Chilton himself is the chief of sinners in this regard, as we shall soon see.

Thomas Walker: "*anything which will make that synagogue-life* [of which Jesus was a product] *better known, may help on to a better understanding of some aspects of the life and teaching of Jesus.*"[40]

---

35. Daniel Boyarin, *The Jewish Gospels: The Story of the Jewish Christ* (New York: New Press, 2012), p. 22.

36. Schalom Ben-Chorin, *Brother Jesus: The Nazarene through Jewish Eyes*. Trans. and ed., Jared S. Klein and Max Reinhart (Athens: University of Georgia Press, 2012), p. 6.

37. Daniel J. Harrington, "The Jewishness of Jesus," p. 125.

38. James H. Charlesworth, *Jesus Within Judaism: New Light from Exciting Archaeological Discoveries*. Anchor Bible Reference Library (New York: Doubleday, 1988), p. xi.

39. Bruce Chilton "Conclusion: Jesus within Judaism," in Chilton, Evans, and Neusner, *The Missing Jesus*, p. 151.

40. Thomas Walker, *Jewish Views of Jesus: An Introduction & an Apprecia-*

Craig Evans: "Jesus in his teaching and behavior is right at home in the world of first century Palestinian Judaism and . . . when placed in his proper context his teaching and behavior make sense."[41] This is circular from the outset: the gospels have already Judaized Jesus, so of course the Jesus based on them is Jewish.

---

tion (New York: Macmillan, 1931), p. 117.

41. Evans, p. 13.

3 CIRCUMCISING JESUS

I want to treat each of several members of the Circumcision party in a little more depth. This will give the reader some idea of how these scholars envision their Rabbi Jesus as well as just what sort of methodology each employs. Often, as we shall see, there is a sizeable dose of imagination, even wishful thinking. See if you agree.

BRUCE CHILTON,
RABBI JESUS: AN INTIMATE BIOGRAPHY.

Like all these books, this one basically takes the Jesus of dogma and tries to give him a human, historical life by clothing him in what we know about life and conditions in first-century Galilee. In effect, "Jesus" *is* Galilee.[42] The whole process, I am thinking, is analogous to what I suspect happened at the start: Paul's celestial Jesus gets historicized by wrapping the Old Testament around him. Chilton continually uses words like "must have" and "would have." It's the same thing William E. Phipps[43] did when he inferred that Jesus must

---

42. "I will be trying to understand the Judaism of Galilean Palestine in the time of Jesus. That does not, of course, give us immediate access to his subjectivity. But if we understand the religious and cultural matrix in which his human consciousness awakened, we know something real about his subjectivity." Lee, *Galilean Jewishness of Jesus*, p. 49.

43. William E. Phipps, *Was Jesus Married? The Distortion of Sexuality in*

have been married since he was called "rabbi" and most rabbis were married.

Chilton builds his portrait on four themes he gratuitously reads into the gospels wherever and whenever he can find (or *create*) an opportunity: first, Jesus was shunned as a *mamzer* (a bastard) and never got over it.[44] Second, he was a Merkavah mystic[45]—and made it central to his message! At any crucial juncture, Chilton's Jesus meditated on his cherished vision of the divine throne-chariot and he taught his followers to do the same. Third, "This is my body/blood" meant he wanted to replace temple sacrifices with raucous, informal banquets![46] Fourth, he was obsessed with "purity" and held the odd view that every Israelite was *ipso facto* "pure"[47] (which seems to verge on E.P. Sanders's controversial view that Jesus never required anyone to repent.[48]) "Purity was Jesus' fundamental commitment, the lens through which he viewed the world."[49] Does Chilton have access to some gospel I don't know about?

Chilton "knows" *way* too much about Jesus' life, thoughts,

the Christian Tradition (New York: Harper & Row, 1970). Another example comes from Dwain Miller, *Jesus the Rabbi: Unlocking the Hebraic Teaching of Yeshua* (Charlotte, NC: LifeBridge Books, 2013), p. 36: "In the pages of Scripture, Jesus was not heard from between age 12 and 30. Why? He was attending rabbinical school. . . . At age 30 He passed the final test and could officially be called, Rabbi Jesus."

44. Chilton, *Rabbi Jesus*, p. 100.

45. Chilton, *Rabbi Jesus*, pp. 50–55, 76, 93, 95, 102, 110, 152–153, 155, 162–163, 192–193, 197, 242–243, 256–257.

46. Chilton, *Rabbi Jesus*, pp. 253–254, 260–261.

47. Chilton, *Rabbi Jesus,* pp. 60, 68–69, 76, 85, 92–93, 122, 140, 144, 171, 185, 192. Amy-Jill Levine, *Short Stories by Jesus: The Enigmatic Parables of a Controversial Rabbi* (New York: HarperCollins, 2014), might well be commenting on this book: "As soon as 'purity' gets on the menu of certain forms of New Testament exegesis, the taste is predictably a bad one, and the food is . . . spoiled" (p. 129).

48. E.P. Sanders, *Jesus and Judaism* (Philadelphia: Fortress Press, 1985), pp. 110–113.

49. Chilton, *Rabbi Jesus*, p. 90.

neuroses,[50] motivations, and what not. Is he reading the Akashic Records? *Rabbi Jesus: An Intimate Biography* reads almost like Anne Catherine Emmerich's fanciful *Dolorous Passion of our Lord Jesus Christ*, even like Bill O'Reilly's novelistic fiasco *Killing Jesus*. What does Chilton think he's doing? He warns us that "Trying to fill in the holes with legends only obscures what we can plausibly surmise."[51] But that's exactly what *he* is doing.

In *Judaism in the New Testament: Practices and Beliefs*, co-authored with Jacob Neusner, Chilton[52] again reads Jesus in light of his "purity" obsession.[53] He shows himself surprisingly gullible, accepting all manner of "Jesus" sayings uncritically. He applies midrashic gimmicks like juxtaposing texts which do not appear to be making his point unless glued together. Incredibly, Chilton takes Acts 15 and 2 Peter as preserving genuine tradition of Simon Peter's Old Testament interpretation.[54] He thinks he knows what Barnabas' approach to Torah, gentiles, etc., was, based on scanty mentions in Galatians— and the apocryphal Epistle of Barnabas.[55] He takes for granted that the Synoptists believed Jesus was God incarnate[56] in service of his schema whereby they expressed their "Judaism" by comparing Jesus to Moses, only with superior divine authority. He misinterprets John 1:51 as Jesus being the new Jacob,[57] whereas it is obviously Nathaniel who is meant. His case that Jesus was a rabbi is about as cogent as his contention that Jesus and the Cypriot Barnabas were boyhood

---

50. Chilton, *Rabbi Jesus*, pp. 103, 104, 179, 181.

51. Chilton, *Rabbi Jesus*, p. 150.

52. Bruce Chilton and Jacob Neusner, *Judaism in the New Testament: Practices and Beliefs* (London and New York: Routledge, 1995).

53. Chilton and Neusner, pp. 123–126.

54. Chilton and Neusner, pp. 109–110.

55. Chilton and Neusner, pp. 116–117.

56. Chilton and Neusner, pp. 130–131.

57. Chilton and Neusner, p. 121.

chums (which he really does say!).[58] Is this cutting-edge New Testament scholarship?

JAMES H. CHARLESWORTH, **JESUS WITHIN JUDAISM**

Charlesworth seems to have Rudolph Steiner-like clairvoyance into the past.

> Stories about what he had said and done were shared by eyewitnesses, who obviously embellished the account but who also had phenomenal *memories*. . . . [Thus] the exegesis of the relevant New Testament passages . . . do[es] not lead to the conclusion that the emotions and enthusiasms of the earliest Christian prophets went unbridled; they were *at least somewhat* controlled by eyewitnesses who anchored enthusiasm in real history.[59]

Did eyewitnesses tell him this?
It only gets worse. Charlesworth says,

> the Gospels are from a later generation than Jesus' own; but, while the evangelists were not eyewitnesses, they were informed by eyewitnesses. Oral tradition is not always unreliable; in fact sometimes it is more reliable than the written word. In the beginning decades of the second century, the careful scholar Papias expressed the need to discover the living oral tradition.[60]

Papias? Really? This is the purveyor of pious absurdities such as that Judas Iscariot outlived Jesus long enough to make a Kong-like spectacle of himself, doubtless sending screaming crowds into the

---

58. Chilton, pp.111–113.

59. Charlesworth, *Jesus Within Judaism*, p. 11.

60. Charlesworth, *Jesus within Judaism*, pp. 19–20.

streets at the sight of him: his head had swollen to the size of a parade balloon so that he could no longer squeeze through street intersections, and that he urinated maggots until, mercifully, he exploded like Mr. Creosote in *Monty Python's The Meaning of Life*. Was Papias to be trusted about Christian origins? Is Charlesworth?

"It is not true that Jesus' sayings were created by the earliest Christians or invented by the evangelists."[61] How, pray tell, does Charlesworth know this? Did his personal savior tell him in a dream? Similarly, Papias, er, I mean, Charlesworth pretends to know that "One of [the major tasks of the early Church] was a concern to remember faithfully something about the precross Jesus."[62] One may apply here Billy Joel's lyric to Charlesworth's labors: "Our graduations hang on the wall, but they never really helped us at all." Even so, for all his erudition, Charlesworth comes across as one more conservative apologist, arguing in a circle that the gospels are based on eyewitness traditions and that embellishments were kept in check under the watchful eyes of eyewitnesses.

He vastly overestimates the importance of the "exciting discoveries" he trumpets. Did we need the Old Testament Pseudepigrapha (hardly recent "discoveries") to tell us apocalypticism was all the rage in Jesus' day? It gets really painful when Charlesworth becomes giddy over the excavation of a house in Galilee that might conceivably have been Peter's domicile. "The first-century house recently excavated at Capernaum beneath the octagonal church of St. Peter may well be the house that Peter owned (Mk 1:29; Mt 8:14–14)." [63] Furthermore, "fishhooks have been found under the pavement of what is identified to be a house-church; hence it is conceivable that a fisherman lived here."[64] "Since there are no rival options for Peter's

---

61. Charlesworth, *Jesus within Judaism*, p. 20.

62. Charlesworth, *Jesus within Judaism*, ibid..

63. Charlesworth, *Jesus within Judaism*, p. 109.

64. Charlesworth, *Jesus within Judaism*, p. 111.

house, and since it was clearly where the house has been discovered or somewhere extremely close to it, it seems valid to conclude that Peter's house may have been excavated and identified. The discovery is virtually unbelievable and sensational."[65] "Peter's house in which Jesus lived when he moved to Capernaum from Nazareth has probably been discovered."[66] Note his rising confidence! This is no more than Easter-season tabloid hype. And note the Albright-ish circularity: we "confirm" the historical accuracy of the Bible by taking it for granted, then finding a possible candidate for some biblical item. I call it "Pin the Tail on the Bible."

"These stone vessels, necessary for purification, are significant for Jesus research." And why is that? "They remind us of the 'six stone jars' prepared 'for the Jewish rites of purification' (Jn. 26), which Jesus reputedly found at the wedding at Cana of Galilee. They raise questions of Jesus' relation to the contemporary heightened laws of purification."[67] What? *How?*

Thomas Kazen, whether or not he had Charlesworth in mind, certainly had his number.

> Influenced by sociology and cultural anthropology, biblical scholars have painted pictures of Jesus as a Galilean cynic, a countercultural sage, a Mediterranean peasant, a marginal Jew, an eschatological prophet, a charismatic healer, a Pharisee, and a rabbi, to name a few. Most of these pictures appeal in one way or another to Jesus' Jewishness. Most of them have been accused of being nothing more than theological constructs. Some more obviously than others seem to suit a modern agenda.[68]

---

65. Charlesworth, *Jesus within Judaism*, ibid.

66. Charlesworth, *Jesus within Judaism*, p. 112.

67. Charlesworth, *Jesus within Judaism*, pp. 107–108. Note, by the way, Charlesworth seems to have no trouble taking for granted that the historical Jesus actually conjured water into wine.

68. Thomas Kazen, "Epilogue. Twenty Years after Sigal: Jesus as Proto-Rabbinic Teacher of Halakhah." In Phillip Sigal, *The Halakhah of Jesus of*

DANIEL BOYARIN,
THE JEWISH GOSPELS

Boyarin is virtually unique in recognizing that early Christian Christology preserves archaic Israelite motifs.[69] But he arbitrarily makes every instance of "Son of Man" a Danielic messianic title (just like George Eldon Ladd),[70] unwisely discounting Vermes's distinctions between references to Danielic visions and euphemistic circumlocutions to oneself or to human beings and their lot in general. Indeed, is he not guilty of what James Barr rightly called "the Kittel fallacy," the erroneous assumption that a particular word means the same thing every time it appears in Scripture?[71] Boyarin thinks Jesus meant to pull rank when he said, "The Son of Man is Lord of the Sabbath" and "The Son of Man has authority on earth to forgive sins." He expected his audience to understand he was claiming to *be* Daniel's "one like a son of man," a second deity beside the Ancient of Days. Surely this is gross over-interpretation of assertions that, as the rabbis also taught, the Sabbath was ordained for the sake of human beings, and that God allows mortal intermediaries to pronounce God's absolution a la *The Prayer of Nabonidus*. Had Jesus spoken of himself as Boyarin thinks he did, he'd have wound up in a straightjacket instead of on a cross.

But if this seems like a camel, it becomes a mere gnat when set beside Boyarin's recapitulation of Stauffer's interpretation of Jesus'

Nazareth according to the Gospel of Matthew. Studies in Biblical Literature Number 18 (Atlanta: Society of Biblical Literature, 2007), pp. 195–196.

69. Boyarin, *Jewish Gospels*, pp. 47–49, 80.

70. Boyarin, pp. 36–38; George Eldon Ladd, *The Presence of the Future: The Eschatology of Biblical Realism* (Grand Rapids: Eerdmans, 1974), p. 214.

71. Named for Gerhard Kittel, editor of *The Theological Dictionary of the New Testament* which took this misleading approach. See James Barr, *The Semantics of Biblical Language* (1961; rpt. Eugene: Wipf & Stock, 2004).

reply to the Sanhedrin: "I am."[72] When Jesus says, "I am," what he means to say is *I am that I am!* This raises all sorts of new exegetical possibilities! "Who's up for some ice cream?" "I am!" "What? You mean you're *Jehovah*? Boy, you sure had *me* fooled, Lord!" (More about Boyarin below.)[73]

BEN F. MEYER,
THE AIMS OF JESUS

Ben Meyer shares with us the good news, as he views it, that:

> Disabused of the artificially misleading impressions occasioned by "apocalyptic" and "messianic secret", we are better positioned to grasp the transparence and coherence of Jesus' career: his proclamation, his teaching, his choice and sending of the twelve, his exorcisms and cures, his table fellowship with the outcast, his demonstration at the temple, his distributing of loaf and cup at the Last Supper.[74]

But everything in this list is historically problematic to say the least. Meyer sloughs off Schweitzer's apocalyptic reading of Jesus even as he champions Jesus as a proclaimer of the imminent arrival of Judgment Day, differing only in the question of whether Jesus urged individuals to repent (Schweitzer's view) or whether Jesus was

---

72. Boyarin, pp. 137–138.

73. Once, at a Society of Biblical Literature conference, I attended a panel discussion in which N.T. Wright, Bernadette Brooten, and others were falling all over themselves praising Boyarin's then-new book *A Radical Jew: Paul and the Politics of Identity* (1997). Over all floated the sense that they knew they had to heap hosannas on a book on Paul written by a Jew. As for Boyarin himself, it was hilarious to see the bemused expression on this humble, unassuming man's face. He looked like he was simply enduring the proceedings.

74. Ben F. Meyer, *The Aims of Jesus.* Princeton Theological Monograph Series 48 (Eugene: Pickwick Publications, 2002), p. 250.

calling for a corporate renewal of the covenant (Meyer's view)—as if that doesn't imply the repentance of all the individuals? He even has his own version of the interim ethic! Meyer says Jesus wanted to end Mosaic legal observance by bringing the commands to their final fulfillment by omitting the commandments' compromises with human hard-heartedness (including Pharisaic mitigations). But this is made possible only by taking the obviously redactional Matthew 5:17 as authentic. Why not rather understand the Matthean Antitheses (Matt. 5:21–48: "You have heard . . . , but I say") as instances of building a fence around the Torah,[75] an emphasis already Jewish?

Meyer himself points out the (supposed) uniqueness of Jesus' fraternization with sinners (though see Schechter on Aaron).[76] Why not go with Jack T. Sanders[77] on this being a legitimation via retrojection of the table fellowship issue in Galatians? As Paula Hendriksen[78] remarks: "It imports Paul and a particular understanding of his mid-first century mission to the Gentiles of the Diaspora back into [the] Palestinian intra-Jewish mission of Jesus." (She is talking about the Pauline notion of Jesus bringing the Law to an end, but her words seem equally applicable to the issue of Jesus' dining with "sinners." She goes further, arguing that much or most of Mark's depictions of

---

75. Solomon Schechter, *Some Aspects of Jewish Theology* (New York: Macmillan, 1910), pp, 212–214.

76. Though see Schechter, p. 321: "We find even that friendly relations were entertained with sinners in the hope that [social!] intercourse with saintly men would engender in them a thought of shame and repentance. Thus it is said of Aaron the High Priest, who 'did turn many from iniquity' (Mal. 2:6), when he met a wicked man he offered him his greetings. When the wicked man was about to commit a sin, he would say to himself, 'Woe unto me, how can I lift my eyes and see Aaron? I ought to be ashamed before him who gave me greetings.' And he would then desist from sin . . . [Similarly, see] the story of R. Zera, who entertained certain relations with the outlaws in his neighbourhood for the same purpose."

77. Jack T. Sanders, *The Jews in Luke-Acts* (Philadelphia: Fortress Press, 1987), pp. 94–96, 134.

78. Paula Hendriksen, *From Jesus to Christ: The Origins of the New Testament Images of Jesus* (New Haven: Yale University Press, 2000), p. 107.

Jesus and his conflicts, etc., are in reality based on situations common in the early church, e.g., the trial before the Sanhedrin, where Jesus is made to represent the "predicted" appearance of his persecuted followers before governors, kings, and synagogue rulers. Ditto dining with (Gentile) sinners. This fits perfectly with Fowler's approach: Jesus is always speaking to the readers, not the intra-diagetic characters.[79]

Ben Meyer is basically a conservative apologist. From the outset he disqualifies critical Jesus studies because of two "errors": denying the possibility of miracles by appeal to the "closed system of cause and effect" (methodological atheism) and the Principle of Analogy.[80]

SEAN FREYNE,
JESUS A JEWISH GALILEAN

This scholar is perhaps the chief of sinners when it comes to making Jesus into the virtual incarnation of Galilee, as if describing the latter is to describe the former. "Captain Galilee." "One is tempted to ask whether Jesus' healing ministry . . . might have given him a special appreciation of the climatic conditions of the Lake area, and the quality of its water, prompting a visit to its source."[81]

> The question has been raised, but to my mind not adequately answered, as to why Jesus' ministry took on a very different style and strategy to that of his erstwhile mentor, John, once he arrived in Galilee. One element of an adequate answer must surely be this shift of environment. . . . The contrast for human living between what the Deuteronomist describes as "the arid wasteland with fiery serpents and scorpions" and "the land with flowing streams

---

79. Robert M. Fowler, *Let the Reader Understand: Reader-Response Criticism and the Gospel* of *Mark* (Minneapolis: Fortress Press, 1991).

80. Meyer, pp. 16–17.

81. Freyne, p. 57.

and with springs and underground waters welling up in valleys and hills" (Deut. 8.7–15; 11,13–17) must have been blindingly obvious. The extent to which such an "exodus" experience might possibly have caused him to reflect again on his understanding of God's call and his own role, especially in the light of the inherited belief in the gift of the land, cannot be properly assessed apart from other aspects of his ministry. Yet, it seems altogether plausible to suggest that the contrasting experience of the *potential blessedness* of life in the land, must have touched him to the point of re-evaluating the present as a graced moment rather than one of awaiting God's imminent judgement, cathartic though the desert environment had been viewed by various Jewish reformers, before and after him.[82]

Poor Freyne! Having spent so much time and effort researching the exciting statistics of the Galilean Agricultural Department Report, he struggles to find, or create, something relevant to historical Jesus studies—unless he is pulling our leg! Again and again Freyne attempts to wring some Jesus-theology out of descriptions of the Galilean terrain[83] usually by way of telepathy. So Jesus visited Gentile Tyre and Sidon . . . think maybe he was considering mounting a Jew/Samaritan ecumenical movement?[84] And did you know Jesus critiqued traditional male roles?[85] Freyne's unrestrained politicizing exegesis, e.g., Jesus' supposed anti-Roman, anti-imperialism a la the People's Front of Judea.[86] For Freyne, Galilee is a burlap canvas onto which he paints a Politically Correct Jesus derived from his fevered imagination.

Freyne, Sanders, Meyer, Chilton, Crossan, and Borg see Jesus as

---

82. Freyne, pp. 42–43.
83. Freyne, pp. 118, 120, 140, 148.
84. Freyne, pp. 110–111, 116.
85. Freyne, pp. 120–121.
86. Freyne, p. 126.

organizing a national movement of renewal. For Freyne, "Jesus enters the region from the desert . . .on a mission to remake [Galilee] in accordance with his vision. . . . It is . . . a challenge to compete for his version of Galilee in relation both to the external and the internal relations that existed in the region."[87] "In calling disciples, and in speaking of them as 'the Twelve', Jesus intended to show that he had in view the full restoration of the people of Israel . . . 'twelve' therefore points to the expectation of an eschatological miracle."[88]

RICHARD A. HORSLEY,
THE PROPHET JESUS
AND THE RENEWAL OF ISRAEL

Horsley takes a similar stance.[89] For him, Jesus was no dreamer spinning fantasies of dragons and sword-bearing angels but rather a prophet in the mould of Elijah and Elisha, seeking to renew his nation by renewing their fidelity to the Mosaic covenant, hence the Torah. He denounced the rulers of his people as corrupt and compromising, both the Pharisees and the Temple hierarchy. He did not predict the miraculous end of the world and of historical existence but rather the historical destruction of the temple and of the Jewish and Roman authorities. The people of Israel would henceforth dwell securely in a kingdom ruled only by Jehovah. They would constitute a new temple, one not erected by any human hand.

Ironically, in this, these cutting-edge scholars have come very close to a maverick form of present-day fundamentalism called

---

87. Freyne, p. 18..

88. E.P. Sanders, *The Historical Figure of Jesus* (New York: Penguin Books, 1995), p. 120. But see p. 178: "in the gospels . . . the only thing that Jesus ever asks people to do is to live right. In none of the material does he urge them to build an alternate society that will be the kingdom of God."

89. Richard A. Horsley, *The Prophet Jesus and the Renewal of Israel: Moving beyond a Diversionary Debate* (Grand Rapids: Eerdmans, 2012).

Preterism,[90] the belief that all apocalyptic language in the Bible was just Technicolor metaphor for intra-historical catastrophic events, whether defeat or victory for the people of God. Did Isaiah and Zechariah actually expect to see the earth scraped clean of human life? Stars crashing into the earth? Multicephalic dragons rising from boiling seas? No, of course not, say Horsley,[91] Sanders, and the Preterists. No, such hyperbole referred to the fall, in war, of oppressive empires, deliverance of righteous Israel/Christians from their persecutors. It is the language of miracle disguising (conveying?) the behind-the-scenes workings of Providence. This view of things comports well with an older theory that apocalyptic texts like Revelation were written in colorful cipher language intended to hide planned political revolutionary actions from the enemies' eyes. Some scholars ascribed literalistic apocalyptic to the "retainer" class, educated scribes who liked to fight the Lord's battles in their imaginations, from the confines (contours) of their comfortable armchairs, while the guys with real guts disdained such Dungeons and Dragons wheel-spinning and preferred to send out assassins and stir up sedition.

But Horsley, Sanders, and their comrades picture Jesus and his disciples (a la Reimarus,[92] Eisler,[93] and Brandon[94]) as real-world ac-

---

90. Charles S. Meek, *Christian Hope through Fulfilled Prophecy: An Exposition of Evangelical Preterism* (Faith Facts Publishing, 2013).

91. Richard A. Horsley, *Jesus and the Spiral of Violence: Popular Jewish Resistance in Roman Palestine* (Philadelphia: Fortress Press, 1993), pp. 133–145.

92. Hermann Samuel Reimarus, *Reimarus: Fragments*. Trans. Ralph S. Fraser. Ed. Charles H. Talbert. Lives of Jesus Series (Philadelphia: Fortress Press, 1970).

93. Robert Eisler, *The Messiah Jesus and John the Baptist according to Flavius Josephus' Recently Rediscovered 'Capture of Jerusalem' and Other Jewish and Christian Sources*. Trans. Alexander Haggerty Krappe (New York: Dial Press, 1931).

94. S.G.F. Brandon, *The Fall of Jerusalem and the Christian Church: A Study of the Effects of the Jewish Overthrow of A.D. 70 on Christianity* (Lon-

tivists (though not necessarily violent). For them as well as others, apocalyptic language/conceptuality served as, so to speak, rallying banners raised high, proclaiming "Conquer by this!" It made sense even if one did not expect a literal incursion of angelic paratroopers onto the field of battle, since it was traditionally believed that Michael and his winged comrades were fighting, unseen by mortal eyes, in the heavens above against the devilish troops of Mordor. The earthly struggle echoed the contest in heaven above.[95]

One might go a step farther to suggest that, when their hoped-for revolution/renewal failed to materialize, they retreated to the pie-in-the-sky alternative of literalist apocalyptic expectation, the last refuge of the helplessly oppressed. This is about the only way I can think of to explain the presence of apocalypse verses alongside "movement" verses in the gospels.

MARCUS J. BORG,
CONFLICT, HOLINESS AND POLITICS
IN THE TEACHING OF JESUS

Borg envisions Jesus as a kind of shaman (plus prophet plus sage) creating a movement of individuals undertaking a mystic (quasi-Buddhistic, quasi-Kabbalistic) experience of ego-death issuing in a conversion experience of selfless compassion. "Holiness was a matter of the heart, for what mattered was a pure heart. The way to purity was not exclusively or even primarily through obedience to the Torah, but the path of dying to the self and the world."[96] This would refocus the national paradigm, rejecting the traditional pursuit of "holiness," dietary and segregational exclusion of "sinners" and of

don: SPCK, 1951).

95. Johannes Weiss, *Jesus' Proclamation of the Kingdom of God*. Trans. and ed., Richard Hyde Hiers and David Larrimore Holland. Lives of Jesus Series (Philadelphia: Fortress Press, 1971), pp. 74–76.

96. Borg, p. 255.

sabbatarianism, in favor of compassionate inclusivity. Borg's Jesus also rejected the ancient faith presumption that God must forever protect his temple and his holy city from conquest by pagans. He pursued this agenda by provoking sabbath controversies by healing people on the sabbath who could easily have waited a day, by openly fraternizing with tax-collectors and sinners, chipping away at the wall of segregationalist holiness that had been erected in order to preserve the holiness of the community of Israel. It was all a strategy to reduce the growing tension with Rome. "The things that make for peace."

It is hard to see how this view is not just a hop, skip, and a jump away from saying that Jesus had rejected the Torah, though Borg insists he didn't. It also comes very close to E.P. Sanders's view that Jesus did not urge repentance. "Jesus was not a preacher of repentance," says Sanders, "he was not primarily a reformer, and in his association with tax collectors he was not trying to persuade them to do what Zacchaeus did."[97] But all this is moot since Borg's whole schema is, first, anachronistic; second, it is never set forth as such but is an abstraction that must be read into individual texts. "The end which he sought was the transformation of the cultural dynamic of the quest for holiness into a cultural dynamic which would conform Israel to God as compassionate."[98]

In that respect it is like the old hybrid pseudo-concept of the combined Suffering Servant/Son of Man (the "Composite Superman").[99] "Assigning a specific reference to them depends upon the overall framework within which the teaching of Jesus is to be explicated, which can be determined only on other grounds."[100] Similarly, it is

97. Sanders, *Historical Figure of Jesus*, p. 230. See Sanders, *Jesus and Judaism*, pp. 203–205.

98. Borg, p. 246.

99. Edmond Hamilton and Curt Swann, "The Origin of the Composite Superman." *World's Finest Comics* # 142, June 1964.

100. Borg, p. 217.

hard to picture in real terms. Did/could Jesus and his disciples have constituted a "peace party"?[101] The "Jesus movement competed with other renewal movements for the loyalty of the Jewish people."[102]

Borg reinterprets various elements in parables and sayings which do not reflect ancient Jewish practice or conditions by introducing data from ancient Judaism that Jesus' hearers "must" have taken for granted, with the result that, e.g., the parables of the Good Samaritan and the Pharisee and the Publican were not about hypocrisy but rather about replacing holiness with compassion.[103] His error is to assume that the gospel writers took all this for granted and left it between the lines. It looks to me like the traditional readings grasp the plain, intended meaning. Maybe the evangelists knew less about ancient Judaism than Borg does.

Amy-Jill Levine[104] criticizes

> the popular academic argument that Jesus offers a "challenge to the purity system of the first-century Jewish social world" and "advocates the politics of compassion in a social world dominated by the politics of purity." The construct is already faulty, since purity and compassion are hardly mutually exclusive. The opposite of compassion is not purity, but lack of compassion. Nor do the Gospels themselves indicate that Jesus's "social world" is "dominated by the politics of purity."[105]

In any case, all this talk of an (organized) "movement" seems to me anachronistic: "If you'd come today you'd have reached a whole

---

101. Gerd Theissen, *Sociology of Early Palestinian Christianity*. Trans. John Bowden (Philadelphia: Fortress Press, 1978), p. 64.

102. Borg, p. 65.

103. Borg, pp. 122–124, 167, 186–188, 206.

104. Amy-Jill Levine, *The Misunderstood Jew: The Church and the Scandal of the Jewish Jesus* (New York: HarperCollins, 2006), p. 146.

105. Quoting Marcus J. Borg, *Meeting Jesus Again for the First Time* (San Francisco: HarperSanFrancisco, 1994), p. 13.

nation. Israel in 4 BC had no mass communication."[106] Were Jeremiah, Isaiah, Amos, Hosea, etc., starting a "movement" or just preaching to the public? I think of evangelist Dwight L. Moody's remark: "God has given me a lifeboat and told me, 'Moody, save all you can!'"

---

106. Judas Iscariot in Tim Rice, "Superstar," in *Jesus Christ Superstar* (MCA Records, 1970).

4 WILL THE REAL JESUS PLEASE START DAVENING?

DAVID DAUBE,
THE NEW TESTAMENT AND RABBINIC JUDAISM

Marcus Borg complains that Bultmann-era scholars assumed that "Disputes about the meaning of the Torah were seen not as going back to Jesus, but as the product of the early Christian movement, necessitated only by the delay of the parousia."[107] But perhaps there were good reasons for this. David Daube offers a couple of examples where the gospel stories of Jesus in dialogue with Jewish scribes conform exactly to the four-fold structure of analogous Rabbinic episodes: "(1) a question by an outsider, (2) a retort good enough for him but not revealing the deeper truth, (3) the request of the disciples, and (4) the full explanation in private."[108] We find this pattern in an anecdote in which a Gentile skeptic accosts Rabbi Johanon ben Zakki, asking why the Jewish ritual of the red heifer is any different from superstitious Gentile magic. The rabbi agrees: there's no real difference. Once the Goy departs, the rabbi's disciples, shocked at their master's reply,

---

107. Borg, *Conflict, Holiness, and Politics*, p. 33.

108. David Daube, *The New Testament and Rabbinic Judaism*. (1956; rpt. Peabody: Hendrickson Publishing, 1998), p. 142.

demand an explanation. He gives an answer he has withheld from the skeptic: the ritual has no intrinsic effect, but one must perform it simply because God has commanded it.

The same thing happens in Mark chapter 7, when some Pharisees demand to know why Jesus' disciples do not observe Pharisaic purity rules by thorough hand washing before meals. Jesus makes a counter-criticism: such ablutions are not stipulated in scripture: it is a recent innovation, which is pretty ironic since the Pharisees have found a loophole whereby, contra scripture, they allow a man to cheat his aged parents out of money he should have set aside to take care of them ("a place for Mom"). And speaking of kosher laws (which they're not exactly doing!) it's pointless anyway since your precious kosher vittles wind up in the same toilet bowl as a ham sandwich! He turns to the crowd and says, "Get this straight, everybody! It's not what goes *into* your mouth that defiles you but what comes *out* of it!" His disciples, indoors, ask for an explanation. Then Jesus gives them the pearls of which he had deemed the pious pigs outside unworthy: It's the poisonous thoughts and hatreds stored inside you that mark you as "unclean," not that shrimp cocktail you had for lunch.

> The Markan description of the dispute concerning divorce is another illustration of the same form. There are four parts: (1) The Pharisees, in whose opinion divorce is permissible, begin the dispute by putting a hostile question. (2) Jesus gives them a mysterious reply, alluding to the creation of the androgynous Adam ('male and female') and to marriage as the re-union of two halves that once belonged together ('they twain shall be one flesh'). The public may or may not guess at the myth referred to; certain it is that they are not supposed to grasp its full implications. (3) At home they receive a clear answer: there can be no valid divorce, and indeed, it is adultery even for a man to remarry after dismissing his first wife—such is the strength of a union making of

husband and wife one composite being.[109]

One might contend that the authentically rabbinical pattern of controversy stories bespeaks an origin with a historical rabbinical Jesus. But is the formal correspondence so exact? Burton L. Mack says, "It was, however, a debate the questioners had no chance to win. Objections are raised in order to set things up for Jesus to win. The objectors get one statement [as in rabbinical dialogues]. Jesus gets at least two pronouncements."[110] Thus the gospel dialogues were obviously the creations of Christians. "[T]he arguments would have been "completely unintelligible for Jews outside the Christian community."[111]

Besides this, we must not ignore all the signs of inauthenticity of the Mark 7 passage. For one, Jesus draws his proof text from the Greek Septuagint, which his Pharisaic opponents would not have deigned to use to wipe their holy hindquarters. A historical Jesus must certainly have quoted the Hebrew Isaiah, only he *wouldn't* have, since the verse in question reads quite differently in the Hebrew original and does not make his point. Nor is Jesus' reply even coherent! Is he talking about ritual hand-washing or about kosher foods? Daniel Boyarin[112] proposes that Jesus meant to reject the Pharisees' policy of extending purity laws to require washing your hands before eating just in case you have somehow incurred ritual contamination, something hardly avoidable unless you stand in the middle of your room all day. But washed hands could not transfer impurity to the food they were about to touch. This is the unstated missing link, Boyarin says, between the Pharisees' question about hand-washing on the one hand and Jesus' fulmination about kosher

---

109. Daube, p. 143.

110. Mack, p. 199, after Jacob Neusner, *Early Rabbinic Judaism*, p. 115.

111. Mack, p. 203, quoting Heinz-Wolfgang Kuhn.

112. Boyarin, pp. 112–116.

food on the other. But it strikes me as if Boyarin knows his Judaism better than Mark did. He is Judaizing Jesus by reading in halakhic technicalities of which Mark would have been oblivious and which are not evident in the words of the text.

The divorce pericope has problems, too. First, Jewish scholars assure us that there was nothing in Jesus' argument to offend the Pharisees because they already recognized the validity of superseding one Torah verse with another, the second essentially negating the first, as Jesus is said to have done by giving God's original plan for marriage (becoming one flesh) precedence over Deuteronomy's allowance of divorce.[113] If this was so, the evangelist has constructed a scene predicated on a misapprehension of Judaism. Second, Daube is able to make the divorce exchange fit the paradigm of scribal debates only by *making* Jesus' initial reply into something sure to puzzle his opponents, and he does this by interpreting it as an ambiguous reference to the myth of Adam beginning as a hermaphrodite (like the Zoroastrian Gayomard). But is that really in view? It looks like a convenient over-interpretation to me. If "Jesus" meant simply that a "match made in heaven" shouldn't be dissolved down on earth, the debate doesn't fit the rabbinical stereotype.

---

113. Phillip Sigal, *The Halakhah of Jesus of Nazareth according to the Gospel of Matthew*. Studies in Biblical Literature No. 18 (Atlanta: Society of Biblical Literature, 2012), p. 86: "a Torah verse could be made inoperative by applying another Torah verse against it." This was a "very rabbinic enterprise." E.P. Sanders, *Jesus and Judaism*, p. 248: "Citing one passage against another in order to justify ignoring or disbelieving an unpalatable part of the Torah is also known. . . . These interpretations, even though the result is to oppose the obvious meaning of a scriptural law, were not considered by those who practiced them to be denials of the law, nor to call into question its adequacy." Geza Vermes, *The Religion of Jesus the Jew* (Minneapolis: Fortress Press, 1993), p. 21: "Nowhere in the Gospels is Jesus depicted as deliberately setting out to deny or substantially alter any commandment of the Torah *in itself*. The controversial statements turn . . . on conflicting laws where one has to override the other."

There is another major reason for rejecting many of the controversy stories, all those that have Jesus defending his healings on the sabbath. Why? Well, it is part of a larger issue.

> The scholarly study of Christian origins has proceeded in terms of critical methods drawn from the humanistic disciplines. The guiding vision, however, has been some imagined event of transformation that might account for the spontaneous generation of the radically new perception, social formation, and religion that Christianity is thought to have introduced to the world. Because this notion of origins has been assumed as self-evident, its derivation from Christian mythology has not been examined. The results of this scholarship, therefore, have been secular apologies [i.e., apologetics] for the truth of the Christian claims to the unique foundations, even though the purpose of the enterprise as a whole has been purportedly self-critical (Burton Mack).[114]

Mack is talking about the tacit assumption that Christianity began with the "Big Bang" of the resurrection (or at least the Easter experiences of the disciples), but the same consideration applies to the healing stories. Supposedly critical scholars are willing to accept them as historically authentic, vaguely granting the possibility of psychosomatic cures like those (supposedly) achieved today. But the exorcisms and cures, together with the mission of the Twelve, fall together because of the obviously fictive feature of Jesus (*and his apprentices!*) being able to perform miracles *on demand* like a comic book superhero. Edward Zeller noticed the problem in one case:

> Immediately after Tabitha's death, Peter is at once summoned from Lydda (verse 38), obviously in the expectation that he will

---

114. Burton L. Mack, *A Myth of Innocence: Mark and Christian Origins* (Philadelphia: Fortress Press, 1991), p. 368.

still bring help. But how could the Christians of Joppa in a natural manner expect such an entirely extraordinary event as the raising of the dead?[115]

All the healing stories, plus the controversy stories based on them, are historically spurious and worthless for establishing a Jesus who carried on halakhic debates with the Pharisees.

HYAM MACCOBY,
JESUS THE PHARISEE[116]

Here the author pursues an agenda familiar from and anticipated in some of his previous work. He aims to separate the historical Jesus from Christianity and to reclaim him for Judaism, hermetically sealing him off from Paul, the real founder of Christianity, an alien religion that has about as much to do with Judaism as the syncretic Sabazian cult did. And, like a recurring video echo on the screen, we can see an ongoing debate between Maccoby and today's preeminent authority on ancient Judaism, Jacob Neusner. It is to Maccoby's credit that he manages to keep the tone of this latter discussion as cordial and collegial as he reminds us the debates among the rabbis were. Though Maccoby finds various minor bones to pick with Neusner, his major gripe is Neusner's notion that Rabbinical Judaism began with Yavne, not with the first-century Pharisee movement, and that the former merely proof-texted the latter, back-dating various traditions, laws, and quotations into the earlier period in order to claim the prestige of the Pharisees for their own, rather different, enterprise. Instead, Maccoby defends the position that the rabbis were the direct successors of the Pharisees (not that there were no inno-

115. Edward Zeller, *The Contents and Origin of the Acts of the Apostles Critically Investigated*. Trans. Joseph Dare Vol. 1 (London: Williams and Norgate, 1875; rpt. Eugene: Wipf & Stock, 2007), p. 271.

116. Hyam Maccoby, *Jesus the Pharisee* (London: SCM Press, 2003).

vations made necessary by changed circumstances), and that Jesus' halakhic positions as recorded in the gospels are so closely parallel to those of the rabbis that he must be considered a prime exemplar of a rabbinical-style Pharisaism that extends back into the first century. As to why the Pharisaic character of the historical Jesus has not been evident from the start, Maccoby takes up the theory he has espoused before, basically that of S.G.F. Brandon, that Jesus viewed himself as King Messiah and hoped to bring about the expulsion of the Romans, albeit by precipitating a divine miracle, not by taking up the sword.

Christians saw the failure of the Jewish Revolt, in which they must have participated, and thereafter they transformed their faith in the fallen Jesus into a purely spiritual salvation cult, under heavy (Pauline-brokered) influence from the Mystery Religions. Seeking to avert Roman hostility, which they and their Master had earned, Christians sought to rewrite history, driving a fictitious wedge between Jesus and Judaism (Pharisaism) already in his lifetime, making him a rejecter of Torah, the very portrait that has served Protestantism so well ever since. This redefinition of Jesus and Christianity entailed the vilification of the Pharisees, originally Jesus' colleagues, casting them as his deadly enemies. The gospels caricature their positions to the point where Jesus is depicted as espousing the actual views of the Pharisees and arguing against bizarre opinions no real Pharisees, as far as we know, ever held.

This effort to reclaim Jesus for Judaism is part of a larger program by which Maccoby seeks to restore Rabbinic (= Pharisaic) Judaism to the place it used to hold in scholarly reckoning as the mainstream of first-century Judaism. Here again Maccoby clashes with Neusner,[117] who has (with others) made clear that the Pharisees, even if they were the major and most popular Jewish sect, were just that: one

---

117. Jacob Neusner, William S. Green, and Ernest Frerichs (eds.), *Judaisms and their Messiahs at the Turn of the Christian Era* (New York: Cambridge University Press, 1987).

Judaism among many. This follows from the cataloguing by Jewish, Christian, and Islamic writers of over a score of Jewish sect names from the early period. Maccoby even resists the conclusions of Jewish scholars who have demonstrated how originally loose-canonical figures like the rain-making hasidim Honi (Onias) the Circle-maker and Hanina ben Dosa were later "rabbinized"[118] (much as Elijah and Elisha were subsequently domesticated by the Deuteronomist Historians).[119] For Maccoby, even John the Baptist was a Pharisee! Here and elsewhere one detects an apologetical agenda on behalf of Rabbinical Judaism analogous to that of N.T. Wright and Luke Timothy Johnson on behalf of conservative Christianity. Of course, that by itself makes no difference; his arguments must stand or fall on their own, no matter how they happened to occur to him or why.

Maccoby calls attention to what seem to him items of data which go against the general redactional/apologetical tendencies of the Hellenizing, Romanizing gospel writers. These he considers loose ends owing their survival to a napping redactor who failed to notice their inimical implications for the case he sought to make. And that, in itself, is sound critical thinking. His favorite example is the caution of Rabban Gamaliel in Acts 5:34–39, according to which the chief of the Pharisees (though Acts doesn't tell us that) sticks up for the early Jewish Christians, entertaining the possibility that their movement might after all be divinely inspired, so that to persecute them might turn out to be opposing God. Maccoby feels that this scene, left intact by Luke, gives the lie to the notion of a Pharisee hatred of

118. William Scott Green, "Palestinian Holy Men: Charismatic Leadership and Rabbinic Tradition" *Aufstieg und Niedergang der römischen Welt* 19/2 (1979), pp. 628–639.

119. Tamis Hoover Renteria, "The Elijah/Elisha Stories: A Socio-cultural Analysis of Prophets and People in Ninth-Century B.C.E. Israel." In Robert B. Coote (ed.) *Elijah and Elisha in Socioliterary Perspective*. Society of Biblical Literature Semeia Studies (Atlanta: Scholars Press, 1992), pp. 75–126; Judith A. Todd, "The Pre-Deuteronomistic Elijah Cycle." In Robert B. Coote (ed.) *Elijah and Elisha in Socioliterary Perspective*. Society of Biblical Literature Semeia Studies (Atlanta: Scholars Press, 1992), pp. 1–36.

Christianity right from the start. And it also means that Christianity cannot yet have contained doctrinal features later repugnant to Judaism, such as divine incarnation, eucharistic blood-drinking, or Torah-apostasy.

The trouble is that (here and elsewhere) Maccoby is entirely too credulous of the texts that come in handy for him. In this case, any historical value of the scene is completely vitiated by the plain fact that it is borrowed lock, stock, and barrel from literary sources. The summary of previous flash-in-the-pan messiahs (Theudas Magus and Judas the Galilean, in that order) comes right out of a too-hasty reading of Josephus,[120] who discussed the two messiahs in reverse order, employing a flashback, which Luke missed. The advice not to persecute the propagators of the new gospel comes straight from Tiresius' warning to Pentheus not to risk opposing God by persecuting Dionysus worship in Thebes, in Euripides' *Bacchae*: "I warn you once again: do not take arms against a god" (lines 789–790).[121] Besides these borrowed elements, there is nothing left. How interesting that Maccoby flatly rejects as a Pauline lie Acts's report that Paul had studied with Gamaliel (Acts 22:3). Too bad he is not as properly skeptical of the earlier Gamaliel mention.

Maccoby similarly takes as history the altercation in Mark 7 over purity laws, maintaining (quite properly) that Jesus is in fact not shown there "declaring all foods clean," since these words are in any case editorial and should probably be read as referring not to "he," Jesus, "declaring" anything, but rather to the latrine which renders all foods clean in the end. The trouble is, the scene is predicated,

---

120. Steve Mason, *Josephus and the New Testament* (Peabody: Hendrickson Publishers, 1992), p. 210.

121. Euripides, *The Bacchae*. Trans. William Arrowsmith. In David Greene and Richard Lattimore, (eds.), *Greek Tragedies Volume 3* (Chicago: University of Chicago Press, 1960), p. 226. Earlier in the play we find a scene closely paralleling Acts 5:34–39, the seer Teiresias warning King Pentheus not to persecute the new religion. Indeed the play is peppered with lines that pop up again, almost verbatim, in Acts.

as we have seen, upon Jesus and Palestinian scribes arguing from the Greek Septuagint, not the Hebrew text of Isaiah. The Hebrew text would not make the point Mark wants his Jesus to make. So the scene cannot very well be a piece of history. Geza Vermes: "since Jesus of Nazareth was a user of the Hebrew Bible and not of the Septuagint, he can in no way be made responsible for the fictitious scripture-based reasoning ascribed to him. In producing this proof, the evangelists had an eye on their Greek readership."[122] In fact,

> it becomes clear that the Old Testament did not play an important role in the preaching of Jesus: he did not argue his doctrine from the Bible. Compared with the Scripture-based teaching style of the Pharisees and the scribes this is quite remarkable. [. .] It would be more correct to speak in these cases of the use of biblical language by Mark, Matthew and Luke than of scriptural citations proper.[123]
>
> So, even if it could be argued that he was so familiar with the scriptures that words of such inconspicuous prophets as Joel or Zephaniah instinctively issued from his lips—and this hypothesis is in no way borne out by the New Testament—the use of implicit quotations cannot be acknowledged as playing a real didactic role and validating in any manner the teachings in which they figure. In fact, there can be hardly any doubt that they owe their existence to the literary/editorial efforts of the evangelists.[124]

Did Jesus believe himself to be the messiah? Maccoby thinks so. But then what about the insight of Wrede[125] and Bultmann:[126] how

---

122. Geza Vermes, *The Authentic Gospel of Jesus* (New York: Penguin Books, 2003), p. 53.

123. Vermes, *Authentic Gospel of Jesus*, pp. 212–213.

124. Vermes, *Religion of Jesus the Jew*, p. 54.

125. William Wrede, *The Messianic Secret*. Trans. J.C.G. Greig. Library of Theological Translations (Greenwood, S.C.: Attic Press, 1971), pp. 216–230.

126. Rudolf Bultmann, *Theology of the New Testament*. Trans. Kendrick Grobel. Scribner Studies in Contemporary Theology (New York: Scribners,

could Jesus have taught his messiahship when the early Christian belief in it was only gradual in dawning, replacing an earlier belief that Jesus had become messiah-designate at the ascension,[127] as well as a second stage whereby Jesus officially became the Messiah as of the resurrection? How can these stages of belief ever have occurred if Jesus had simply taught (even privately) that he was already the Messiah?

Maccoby is even willing to accept Matthew's amplification of Mark's (already fictive—see Gerd Thiessen)[128] Caesarea Philippi scene in which Jesus bestows vizier-like powers upon Peter, the keys of the kingdom. This will come in handy to explain that Peter was subordinate, in the reckoning of Jesus himself, to James, Jesus' regent in the Jerusalem caliphate. Maccoby needs the structures and beliefs of Jerusalem Christianity to go back to Jesus, not to be merely one of several mutations of Jesus-faith after his death. But he is building upon pretty sandy soil.

In just the same way, Maccoby mounts a doomed argument that Matthew 5:17 and 19 represent an authentic saying of Jesus, who therefore must have envisioned no Pauline-style abrogation of the Torah. Now it is clear that the underlying Q saying Matthew 5:18 (also Luke 16:17) does mean to attribute just such a position to Jesus (whether correctly or not, who knows?). But it seems impossible not to take the adjacent verses as Matthean embellishment. That they cannot go back to Jesus in any case is evident from the fact that verse 17 already knows of a rival *Christian* opinion that Jesus "came to" abolish the scriptures, theological language interpreting the ministry

---

1951, 1955), vol. 1, pp. 26–32.

127. John A.T. Robinson, "The Most Primitive Christology of All?" In Robinson, *Twelve New Testament Studies*. Studies in Biblical Theology 34 (London: SCM Press, 1962), pp. 139–153.

128. Gerd Theissen, *The Miracle Stories of the Early Christian Tradition*. Trans. Francis McDonagh (Philadelphia: Fortress Press, 1983), pp. 171.

of Jesus, a figure of the past. Jesus cannot have said this.[129]

Matthew 23:1–2, where Jesus urges his disciples to accept all the teachings of the scribes and Pharisees, though not to emulate their personal conduct, as they do officially occupy "Moses' seat," falls prey to archaeology, for the Cathedra of Moses was a literal throne in the chancel of the synagogues—of the second century, not the first. But Maccoby ascribes the whole business to Jesus, who therefore must have been an orthodox Pharisee.

Maccoby claims Matthew 9:10–13 as a rare glimpse of Jesus' true regard for his Torah colleagues: if he were to spend his time with them he would be like a physician spending all his time at the AMA while neglecting his sick patients. Thus Jesus must have regarded the Pharisees as the "righteous who need no repentance." But why should we assume the Pharisees are in view? What Jesus' critics want to know is why Jesus consorts with a bad element instead of with upstanding folks. Neither they nor he say anything implying the "righteous" are the Pharisees.

In order to salvage such friendly but dubious texts from the cutting-room floor, Maccoby proposes to go John Dominic Crossan one better and to extend the latter's criterion of multiple attestation, in other words, to make the holes in the net wider so more fish can make it through. In company with other form-critics, Crossan had proposed accepting the authenticity of any saying that was to be found in two or three unrelated early Christian sources, say Mark and Q. Maccoby says that we ought to include sayings that appear even in related sources, like all three Synoptics. Why? Apparently because Matthew and Luke could have edited a Markan saying had they wanted to, and the fact that they left it alone must mean they set their imprimatur on it. But this is to misunderstand the nature of redaction criticism. All it means for Matthew and Luke to have left Mark alone is that they did not see the Markan material as under-

---

129. Bultmann, *History of the Synoptic Tradition*, p. 155.

mining the new emphases they wanted to add. It has nothing to do one way or the other with how accurate a reporter Mark was.

Maccoby rightly sees in the gospels a polemic against the Pillars/ Heirs of Jesus and the Jerusalem Christianity they headed. He echoes F.C. Baur[130] (whom otherwise he excoriates), Ernst Käsemann,[131] and Oscar Cullmann[132] in seeing the significance of the fact that the Sanhedrin's persecution of Hellenistic Stephen-Christianity left the Twelve unmolested (Acts 8:1). Surely this means that there were two very different kinds of Christianity struggling in the Jerusalem womb, and that the Sanhedrin saw nothing particularly objectionable in that headed by the Twelve. But Maccoby dismisses as absurd Baur's conjecture that Jerusalem Christianity had "re-Judaized" the more radical, less nationalist, Torah-indifferent gospel of the historical Jesus. It seems obvious to Maccoby that if Jesus' own brothers (James the Just and, after him, Simeon bar Cleophas) led the Jerusalem faction, aided by the Twelve, their version of the faith must stem from Jesus himself. And that does make sense on the surface. But one ought not neglect possible historical analogies to the development as Baur pictured it. For instance, the eighteenth-century Hasidic movement begun by the Baal Shem Tov was at first anti-legalistic, disdaining the letter in favor of the Spirit. They denounced what they perceived as fossilized rabbinical orthodoxy. But it was not long before they shed this radicalism and became some of the most zealous students of Torah and Talmud. It is natural to understand

---

130. Ferdinand Christian Baur, *Paul the Apostle of Jesus Christ: His Life and Works, His Epistles and Teachings.* Trans. A. Menzies. Two volumes (London: Williams & Norgate, 1873–1875; rpt. Peabody: Hendrickson Publishers, 2003), pp. 39–41.

131. Ernst Käsemann, *Jesus Means Freedom: A Polemical Survey of the New Testament.* Trans. Frank Clarke (London: SCM Press, 1969), p. 46.

132. Oscar Cullmann, "Dissensions within the Early Church." In Richard Batey (ed.), *New Testament Issues.* Harper Forum Books (New York: Harper & Row, 1970), pp. 119–129. See also Hans-Joachim Schoeps, *Jewish Christianity, Factional Disputes in the Early Church.* Trans. Douglas R.A. Hare (Philadelphia: Fortress Press, 1964), pp. 5–6.

Jesus this way, as Geza Vermes[133] and others do. Suppose he was like the Galilean hasids who performed miracles and yet sat loose to the niceties of the Law, for which laxity they received scorn from the Pharisees. Not coincidentally, Maccoby has already challenged Vermes's reconstruction of the hasids as a possible precedent for a non-legalistic Jesus. It is a strategic move, eliminating a dangerous chess piece from the board before one's opponent can use it.

Also, one might posit that the very same survival instinct evidenced in the Pauline/Markan Christian attempt to Romanize Christianity in order to avert Roman persecution had earlier led to Jewish Christians jettisoning the radicalism of Jesus in order to buy the very toleration by the Sanhedrin that Maccoby rightly indicates that they enjoyed.

There is another thought-provoking parallel farther afield. I am thinking of what happened in India in the aftermath of the Upanishadic revelation. Kshatriya sages, weary of the ritual formalism and the caste domination of the priestly Brahmin elite, sought the solitude of the forests to meditate. Looking within, they realized the invisible power thought to reside in the Vedic rituals performed by the priests, a power called the Brahman, was instead located in the innermost self, the *atman*, of every sentient being. The only requisite "sacrifice" was that of the introspective heart. This conclusion would seem to have rendered the whole Vedic system obsolete, and so most of the priests opposed it. But some Brahmins liked what they heard, and they decided it must actually constitute the esoteric truth of the Vedas, not a repudiation of them. So, while many Kshatriyas, like the Buddha and Mahavira, flatly rejected the Vedic scriptures and rituals, and most Brahmins rejected the Kshatriya heresy, there were some Brahmins who "re-Vedicized" the new doctrine, writing massive commentaries (Brahmanas, Aranyakas, Upanishads) on the Ve-

---

133. Vermes, *Jesus the Jew: A Historian's Reading of the Gospels* (Glasgow: Fontana/Collins, 1976), chapter 3, "Jesus and Charismatic Judaism," pp. 58–82.

das, expounding them in accord with the new revelation, actually filling the old skins with new wine and holding them together as best they could.[134] Is that not how Mark 2:18, 21–22 sees the matter? Not that it's necessarily correct.

Maccoby rejects another Judaism-Hinduism parallel that has become practically an axiom of Politically Correct Jesus scholarship over the last couple of decades. Many have grossly misconstrued the notion of Jewish purity laws as if they established socio-economic caste divisions within Jewish society in Jesus' day. The gospel "sinners" were, we are often told, whole professional classes whose members were stuck in a perpetual state of ritual uncleanness because their work involved constant contact with the dead, with wounds, animal carcasses, etc. As a result, the historical Jesus can be depicted as a first-century Gandhi, seeking out the Shudras and the Untouchables and declaring them *harijans*, children of God. This, for instance, is the party-line view of Jesus propagated by television documentaries and the talking heads they interview. Jesus as Dr. King. One hesitates to say it, but it looks like Liberal Protestantism, unsatisfied with a Jesus who is a relic of ancient concerns and debates, is remodeling Jesus after modern heroes whom they would really prefer. In short, they do not make Gandhi and Dr. King into Christ figures, but rather they make Jesus into a Gandhi figure or a King figure. Maybe they should just be up front about it and set up a new religion based on the Mahatma and Dr. King. Many of us would join up.

Maccoby is right: what these perilous modernizers of Jesus miss is that purity laws did not forbid all acts incurring impurity. Instead, they took for granted that many needful acts regularly incurred ritual impurity and stipulated what to do to negate it, sometimes washing your hands, sometimes just waiting till sundown, etc. Undertakers might find themselves "unclean" more of the time than other folks, but it was absolutely necessary, and a major charitable

---

134. Paul Deussen, *The Philosophy of the Upanishads*. Trans. A.S. Geden (1906, rpt. New York: Dover Publications, 1966), pp. 19–23.

act, to wash and bury the dead. And to recognize this obvious fact (at least it *should* have been obvious)[135] is to stultify all those chic interpretations that Jesus was courageously and "radically" reversing contemporary norms when he allowed lepers or menstruating women to touch him. As Maccoby says, no such issues are mentioned in the narrative. They have to be read in by modern exegetes who sometimes seem to know *too* much about the background of this or that pericope. The gospel writers seem to be unaware of such factors, either because we have got the facts wrong, or *they* did, writing far away from the Palestine of the first third of the first century CE..

At first Maccoby himself seems to fall victim to the same error when he discusses Jesus' defense of his disciples' gleaning on the sabbath (Mark 2:23–26) by an appeal to the scriptural precedent of David, on the run from Saul, feeding his famished men with the reserved sacrament (1 Sam. 21:1–6). Maccoby notes the silliness of the reply if all Jesus was defending was his disciples' convenience. The Davidic case would be relevant only if they were in danger of *starving*. So maybe they *were*: perhaps the story silently presupposes that Jesus and his lieutenants are on the run from a persecuting Herod, their lives in danger as rebels, just like David and his men. At first one thinks: Maccoby is reading in a concern of which the text seems innocent. But no. What he is doing is applying to a puzzling narrative a paradigm which has proven quite productive in solving other such puzzles. Suppose the narrative, which makes little sense as it stands, is missing something that would make sense of it, but which would be too dangerous to say aloud. On the Brandon hypothesis, we can readily imagine the censoring of precisely this element of explanation: Jesus and his men were in genuine need because of political persecution, the kind he is now in retrospect never supposed to have undergone. It is one of Maccoby's many fresh insights. However, one

---

135. Thankfully, it *is* readily apparent to E.P. Sanders, *Jesus and Judaism*, pp. 182–184.

still needs to take into consideration Bultmann's insight[136] that the text shows scribes questioning and Jesus defending the actions *not of Jesus but of his disciples,* i.e., of early Christians, and that this implies the pericope, together with the issue itself, arose post-Jesus. It is not evidence for the historical Jesus after all.

I have already called attention to Maccoby's twin goals of defending Rabbinic Judaism as the direct continuation of Pharisaism and of establishing Jesus as a typical first-century Pharisee. For both purposes he needs to discount Neusner's argument, confessedly learned from Bultmann, that one cannot trust rabbinical/redactional ascriptions of oft-recurring sayings to any particular name.[137] If a saying is ascribed to Rabbi A in this document but to Abba B in that one, we must approach the ascriptions synchronically, not diachronically. What function does a particular ascription serve in the document in which we find it? Presumably there will be different purposes behind different attributions. And neither will necessarily be merely one of historical inquiry. Maccoby does not like this kind of talk.[138] For him, attributions must be taken seriously, and this means the traditions of the rabbis are rooted squarely in the soil of first-century Pharisaism. Yet Maccoby feels free to disregard rabbinical ascriptions when he reasons that, if a Jesus parable sounds like a rabbinical parable first attributed to a rabbi living centuries after Jesus, it may yet be much older, already available for Jesus to have borrowed. (Jeremias thought the same thing.)[139] Sure, a parable may first appear in a later rabbinic source, but that only means that the disciple attributed the parable

---

136. Bultmann, *History of the Synoptic Tradition*, p. 16.

137. Jacob Neusner, *The Peripatetic Saying: The Problem of the Thrice-Told Tale in Talmudic Literature.* Brown Judaic Studies 89 (Chico: Scholars Press, 1985); Neusner, "Rabbinic Biography: Exemplary Pattern in Place of Lives of Sages" *Journal of Higher Criticism* (11/2) Fall 2005, pp. 9–13.

138. Maccoby, p. 209.

139. Joachim Jeremias, *The Parables of Jesus* (New York: Scribners, 2nd rev. ed., 1963), p. 178–179.

to the master from whom he had initially heard it, not that he has ascribed it to its actual originator.[140] But doesn't this land Maccoby in a fatal contradiction? Surely, given the tradition-oriented character of rabbinical learning, a disciple would have heard the parable (or other saying) *as attributed to its ostensible originator*. His own master would have said, "Rabbi So-and-so used to say . . ." If, then, a saying or parable meets us attributed first to a later figure, we have no right to back-date it to Jesus' day. Rather, we must take the rabbinical parable as the source of the gospel parable (provided the gospel version appears to be later, e.g., garbled) and *admit it is anachronistic for Jesus*. And remember, we have no right to date the gospel version as older than the earliest manuscript or patristic citation in which we find it.

Neusner, then, suggests that sayings which originated later have been retrojected into the mouths of more ancient sages, to give the sayings added antiquity and authority. He infers this, I think, from the fact that, were the saying known to stem from the earlier author, we would never find it attributed also to a later one. If it were known to have come from first-century Rabbi A, who would ever have ascribed it instead to the less authoritative because more recent Abba B? This seems sound critical thinking to me. And thus Maccoby is not merely inconsistent but wrong as well. The Maccoby who implicitly agrees with Neusner that an attribution to an earlier source (e.g., to Jesus) as its originator may be fictive is right. The Maccoby who rejects the same Neusner axiom (when it comes to first-century Pharisees) is wrong.

Throughout the book one anticipates seeing Maccoby say something about an earlier book with the same title, *Jesus the Pharisee* by Harvey Falk,[141] who argued pretty much the same case. In fact,

---

140. Maccoby, p. 93.

141. Harvey Falk, *Jesus the Pharisee: A New Look at the Jewishness of Jesus* (Mahwah: Paulist Press, 1985).

Maccoby for some reason[142] never mentions him by name, though he does at length reject an important piece of Falk's argument. Like Falk, Maccoby is busy demonstrating that virtually every halakhic judgment ascribed to Jesus in the gospels is attested also for more or less contemporary Pharisees. Where they differ is that Falk sees Jesus being depicted as a liberal rabbi in the tradition of Abba Hillel, pursuing a policy of leniency that brought him into fatal collision with the Pharisees of Shammai's more severe faction. Maccoby, on the other hand, points out that the gulf between the factions of Hillel and Shammai was not that wide, and that, at least on divorce, Jesus is shown as closer to Shammai than to the easy-going Hillel.

Maccoby seems to step beyond all possible evidence and to betray the wishful character of his project when he gratuitously asserts that John and Jesus "were regarded by the Pharisees as well-meaning, loyal, and breathtakingly courageous Jews, making claims that had an honored place in tradition and would someday be fulfilled, even if the present claimants, like so many before them, turned out to be disappointments."[143] Cf. David Flusser: "the Pharisees regarded the handing over of Jesus to the Romans as a repulsive act of sacerdotal despotism."[144] Here we have supposition made into fact, the same process by which the fictive gospel tradition grew in ancient times. Not only that, but we also have a prime case of the very "re-Judaization" process against which Maccoby himself rails.

---

142. Probably because Falk's discussion pays virtually no attention to New Testament scholarship and takes a largely uncritical approach to Jewish traditions crucial to his case. See Jacob Neusner, *Rabbinic Literature & the New Testament: What We Cannot Show, We Do not Know* (Valley Forge: Trinity Press International, 1994), p. 96.

143. Maccoby, p. 66.

144. Flusser, p. 49.

SHMULEY BOTEACH,
KOSHER JESUS[145]

Boteach's book is largely an (acknowledged) rehash of the work of
Hyam Maccoby, especially of the latter's *Revolution in Judea, The
Mythmaker,* and *Judas Iscariot and the Myth of Jewish Evil.* There is
really nothing new in it. *Kosher Jesus,* so dependent on Maccoby's
work, inherits his most serious flaws as well. Boteach shows only
the vaguest acquaintance with the results of biblical criticism. He
assumes the historicity of Moses and that the oral traditions of the
scribes really do all go back via oral transmission to him. For Boteach, King David actually composed the Psalms. He even supposes
that Simon Peter is the author of the apocryphal gospel bearing his
name! Hoo boy. Maccoby was not guilty of those sins, but he did assume that the epistles ascribed to Paul, as well as the speeches he is
shown giving in Acts, are primary sources usable to determine what
the Apostle to the Gentiles believed and taught. Thus much of the
reconstructions of Paul and his role by Maccoby and Boteach turn
out to be a castle erected upon sand.

But it seems to me that the biggest problem with *Kosher Jesus* is a
fault line threatening to rupture his portrait of Jesus. Boteach imag-
ines Jesus as a dyed-in-the-wool Pharisee who freshened Judaism
and treasured the compassion of a loving God.[146] Yet Boteach's Jesus
is also something of a Mr. Hyde, a militant rabble-rouser dripping
with venomous loathing for the Romans, against whom he incites
violent revolution.

> With remarkable courage, he rises up and publicly decries the
> Romans. . . . He inspires the wary Jews to overcome their fears
> of Rome. He broadcasts his call to arms far and wide, building a

---

145. Shmuley Boteach, *Kosher Jesus* (Jerusalem: Gefen Publishing
House, 2012).

146. Boteach, p. 4.

passionate and devoted following. The teacher's rhetorical style is eclectic, complementing homespun parables with fierce fighting words to inspire in his listeners a craving for rebellion. If the Jews reassert their true fidelity to God, he says, they will be victorious. All of Rome's legions cannot overcome the Rock of Israel. Had God not destroyed the chariots of Pharaoh? Had he not helped David defeat Goliath? Had he not slaughtered Sennacherib's legions in their thousands when they camped outside Jerusalem? He will do so again.[147]

I do not see, first, where Boteach gets all his "information" about Che Jesus, and, second, how he can reconcile the two Jesuses implied in his reconstruction. Of course he must and does claim that the anti-Roman preaching has been censored by later redactors of the gospels (implying earlier versions which portrayed a bloodthirsty Jesus?) and replaced with teaching befitting a Harold Kushner Jesus, a Leo Buscaglia Jesus. Evan Moffic[148] comments: "Unfortunately, some of . . . Boteach's focus on Jesus the zealot and national hero obscures the universalism of his teachings." But Boteach still wants Jesus to have imparted the sweet and saintly Sermon on the Mount. So he must think Jesus was both Jekyll and Hyde—at the same time! Good luck with that one!

It is notable that Boteach's Jesus is the diametrical opposite of Marcus Borg's. Perhaps more importantly, Boteach's picture of Jesus calls into question the scenario envisioned by S.G.F. Brandon, who also considered Jesus to be an armed revolutionist. Brandon built his case by connecting several dots that are naturally read as loose ends, vestiges of an otherwise-effaced original account of the Zealot Jesus. But Brandon left it to the historical imagination as to what his Jesus

---

147. Ibid.

148. Evan Moffic, *What Every Christian Needs to Know about the Jewishness of Jesus: A New Way of Seeing the Most Influential Rabbi in History* (Nashville: Abingdon Press, 2015), p. 172.

might have been heard to preach. And Boteach, as quoted just above, has obviously let his imagination fill that gap, making Jesus sound like a wild-eyed Cargo Cult prophet. Is the bulk of Synoptic gospel teaching *all* whitewash?

> Some scholars have seen . . . evidence that Jesus was himself in-volved in political messianism of the sort associated with Judah the Galilean or Bar Kochba; but unless we discount the irenic and politically nonconfrontational traditions in the gospels and Paul as protective camouflage vis-à-vis Rome, this seems unlikely. (Paula Fredriksen).[149]

But maybe so! After all, that would seem to be implied in the work of the form-critics, who saw almost all gospel sayings and sto-ries as church creations. Oscar Cullmann remarked:

> It is clear that the proponents of the thesis that Jesus was a rev-olutionary, and those of the thesis that he was, on the contrary, a defender of the existing order, must exclude either the one or the other group of sayings and narratives of Jesus. There is a very simple means for accomplishing this: One suppresses those which contradict the thesis which one supports himself.[150]

Boteach explains why Jews did not and still do not accept Jesus as the Jewish Messiah: he was unable to bring about the Kingdom of God, the end of Rome, the Final Judgment, etc. But he does offer a positive estimate of Jesus. For him, Jesus was not a *false* Messiah but rather a *failed* Messiah. He urges Jews to recognize Jesus as a martyred hero, not a seducer of Israel. Jesus, then, would be another

---

149. Fredriksen, *From Jesus to Christ*, p. 120.

150. Oscar Cullmann, *Jesus and the Revolutionaries*. Trans. Gareth Put-nam (New York: Harper & Row, 1970), p. 10.

Simon bar Kochba, not another Sabbatai Sevi or Jacob Frank.[151]

BRAD H. YOUNG,
JESUS THE JEWISH THEOLOGIAN[152]

This tome promises much but delivers little. We cannot, he saith, even begin to understand Jesus without plumbing the depths of Rabbinic/Pharisaic Judaism, in the light of which Jesus *must* be interpreted. Never mind that the book is maddeningly repetitive and that every other word is "rich." One problem is that he is largely recycling the work of David Flusser[153] with whom he studied in Jerusalem. Young is an Evangelical Protestant on the faculty of Oral Roberts University and therefore takes a completely uncritical view of narratives in the gospels. Jesus, he "thinks," did say everything ascribed to him in the text. And so Young is like a detective wearing a blindfold. He has expended vast time and energy to familiarize himself with Hebrew and with rabbinical sources, but to no real profit. There are Jewish parables and parallels aplenty, but mostly they just serve to add "local color" in the manner of popular works like *Halley's Bible Handbook*. You know, "background." The edifying homiletics

151. See the discussion of this proposal, originally that of Irving Greenberg, in Steven Leonard Jacobs, "Can We Talk? The Jewish Jesus in a Dialogue between Jews and Christians," in Zev Garber, ed., *The Jewish Jesus: Revelation, Reflection, Reclamation* (West Lafayette: Purdue University Press, 2011), pp. 345–357; Shaul Magid, "The New Jewish Reclamation of Jesus in Late Twentieth-Century America: Realigning and Rethinking Jesus the Jew," in Zev Garber, pp. 358–382; Moffic, *What Every Christian Needs to Know*, pp. 174–176; Byron L. Sherwin, "'Who Do You Say that I Am?' (Mark 8:29): A New View of Jesus." In Beatrice Bruteau, ed. *Jesus Through Jewish Eyes: Rabbis and Scholars Engage an Ancient Brother in a New Conversation* (Maryknoll: Orbis Books, 2001), pp. 36–44.

152. Brad H. Young, *Jesus the Jewish Theologian* (Grand Rapids: Baker Academic, 1995).

153. Oral tradition from my professor, David M. Scholer, tells that Flusser once remarked that, if the Jewish Messiah, when he arrives, turns out to be Jesus, it would be all right with him.

that take up so much of the book reek of the smarmy "discipleship" bromides of suburban megachurches and TV preachers. Young had little problem studying with David Flusser, who had a similarly uncritical approach to gospel narrative: "Nothing that we have learned casts any doubt upon the historicity of Jesus' experience at his baptism in the Jordan."[154] Flusser's methodology, if one can call it that, must be called oracular: "Buber once said, in a conversation, that if a man has the gift of listening, he can hear the voice of Jesus himself speaking in the later accounts of the Gospels. This authentic note can, I believe, be detected in Jesus' comments concerning the Baptist [Matt. 11:7–15]. These are at once simple and profound, naïve and full of paradox, tempestuous and yet calm."[155] Again, "Matthew's version of Jesus' address to Peter [Matt. 16:17–19] has an authentic ring about it."[156]

Young simply presupposes the orthodox Jewish identity of Jesus. He speaks of "Jesus' training and experience as a learned teacher of Torah,"[157] an estimation not shared by John's gospel (John 7:15, "The Jews marveled at it, saying, 'How is it that this man has learning, when he has never studied?'"). Deductively, Young presumes to describe Jesus' religious practices. "Such blessings are used during meals. Certainly Jesus *would have* employed these same blessings with his disciples."[158] Similarly, Jacques Baldet: "Jesus also prayed at the synagogue, . . . probably going there every day of the week."[159] If Jews did it, Jesus did it. Can we take it for granted that Jesus ate

---

154. Flusser with R. Steven Notley, *The Sage from Galilee: Rediscovering Jesus' Genius* (Grand Rapids: Eerdmans, 2007), p. 22.

155. Flusser, p. 30.

156. Flusser, p. 109.

157. Young, p. xxxiv.

158. Young, p. 121, emphasis mine.

159. Jacques Baldet, *Jesus the Rabbi Prophet: A New Light on the Gospel Message*. Trans. Joseph Rowe (Rochester, VT: Inner Traditions, 2005), p. 74.

knishes, too? "Rabbi Akiva taught, 'A person is forbidden to taste anything before saying a blessing over it.' Before eating, Jesus surely *would have* said a blessing."[160] I think of a halakhic joke in which two rabbis are searching for some scriptural mandate justifying the wearing of yarmulkes. One says, "How about *this* verse!" His colleague reads it: "'And Abraham went out from there.' So *what*?" The first replies triumphantly, "Would Abraham go out without his yarmulke?"

The whole thing is completely circular. Likewise, Young assures us that the gospel Jesus sayings are authentic because, as per rabbinic practice, the rabbis had their students memorize them so they could pass them down to their own students. Well, that's fine—*if* we already know Jesus was a standard-brand rabbi, which is the very point of contention. In broader terms, this book shares with others more sophisticated, the circularity of making the historical-Jewish Jesus pretty much a function, an instantiation, of all the data we can gather about first-century Galilee: whatever it was, he was. "The more we learn about this fascinating period of history, the more we will know about Jesus."[161] Likewise Flusser: "the Synoptic Gospels, if read through the eyes of their own time, still portray a picture of Jesus as a faithful, law-observant Jew."[162] Naturally, if you look through a colored lens, everything you see will seem to be that color.

But the surest sign that Young is in fact Judaizing Jesus is his habit of reinterpreting gospel parables by reading into them rabbinic beliefs or rules unmentioned in the texts, and so twisting what seems the straightforward sense of the parable. Jesus, you see, must have known as much of Rabbinics as Young does. Similarly, he tries to exorcize the Zealot spirit from the Q saying "The kingdom of God advances violently and the violent seize it by force" by referring back to an obscure scribal midrash on Micah 2:13 ("The breaker who opens

---

160. Young, p. 123, emphasis mine.

161. Young, p. xxxiv.

162. Flusser, p. 35.

the breach rises up before them") which takes it as a prediction that King Messiah's forerunner would break through a stone wall so his Lord could enter and conquer. So, Young argues, Jesus meant to say that the breaker was John the Baptist opening the way for Jesus to bring forth the kingdom of God.[163] Nice try, Brad. He is rewriting the gospel text in light of Rabbinic midrash, not illuminating the former by the latter.

Usually, though, the vaunted rabbinic background adds nothing to the familiar modern interpretations of the passage Young discusses. For example, everyone "knows" that the Matthean parable of the Workers in the Vineyard teaches that God does not exactly reward an individual's righteousness but instead showers the same saving grace upon all his servants/believers. If you grouse about that, you're just as "selfish" as the complainers in the parable.[164] Young invokes the rabbinic "parallel" concerning the eulogy for the 28 year old prodigy Rabbi Bun bar Hijja. Why did God cut him off prematurely? The parable has a landowner send laborers into his field, but, after a measly couple of hours, he tells one harvester to quit work and stroll around shooting the breeze with the boss while the rest of the laborers sweat all day. At quitting time the man who was pulled off the line early gets as much pay as the rest, who start griping at the seeming injustice.[165] The boss, implicitly rebuking them, explains that the favored worker had already done, in a mere two hours, more

---

163. Young, pp. 51ff.

164. Wouldn't the parable make more sense if the landowner told his later recruits in advance that he would give them the full amount no matter how short their workday turned out to be? If he promised them only a fraction of a workaday wage, would they think it worthwhile? Maybe he knew he'd have to promise them the full wage in order to get any takers.

165. Something similar occurs in an episode of The Sopranos ("Unidentified Black Males," Season 5, episode 9, May 2, 2004) in which, upon learning that one of the guys on the construction site is the boyfriend of Tony's daughter Meadow, Paulie Walnuts tells the young man to drop his work and relax with the other Mafiosi in the cool shade. (Okay, so it's irrelevant. I love parallels.)

than any of the rest of them had done in a full day! Despite the superficial resemblance, the point is quite different from Matthew's parable: it is a matter, not of the boss's generosity but rather of "quality versus quantity" (cf. 1 Cor. 15:10). Thus Young's invoking a rabbinic "parallel" fails.

Young, basically a sophisticated fundamentalist, naturally cannot abide Rudolf Bultmann and form-criticism, and this prevents him from recognizing the plausible (I should say obvious, once you know anything about form-criticism, which Young appears not to) meaning of this parable and others like the Prodigal Son, both of which seem to make perfect sense as having originated post-Jesus in the conflict described in Acts 10–11 over the propriety of the Gentile Mission, in which Jewish-Christian elders begrudged the equal status accorded to Johnny-come-lately Gentile converts.[166] Or, if one prefers the equally cogent view of Joachim Jeremias, that, if authentically from Jesus, these parables defended Jesus' outreach to sinners thought to be beyond the pale. But, wait a second, weren't the Pharisees happy to see a sinner repent? "Who were those Jews who opposed the offer of grace to sinners?" (E.P. Sanders).[167] "It is simply inconceivable that Jewish leaders would have been offended if people repented."[168] If we insist otherwise, then we have another example of gospel authors not knowing what they were talking about. But even Young is willing to grant that you could have found the occasional hypocrite among his idealized Pharisees.

---

166. Sanders, *Jews in Luke*-Acts, p. 107–108. Schalom Ben-Chorin gets it exactly backwards: "The older brother is not, as many Christian interpreters presume, a kind of representative of the synagogue, nor does the younger brother represent the pagan-Christian church that found its way out of squalor to the God of Israel. Such an interpretation would mean that this parable belongs to a much later kerygma and therefore lacks authenticity. I believe instead that it entails a variation on a rabbinical principle," etc. (*Brother Jesus: The Nazarene through Jewish Eyes*. Trans. and ed., Jared S. Klein and Max Reinhart (Athens: University of Georgia Press, 2012), pp. 78–79.

167. Sanders, *Jesus and Judaism*, p. 40.

168. Sanders, *Jesus and Judaism*, p. 272.

Like other scholars we are discussing, Young tends to take problematic gospel verses which, on a straight reading, seem not to jibe with modern knowledge of ancient Judaism and to explain them away by supplying dubiously relevant halakhic details, reading them into the gospel text. Is not the more natural inference that our evangelists were not so well informed about Judaism, and even that the stories, predicated on misunderstandings of Jewish law and custom, are sheer fiction? They're trying to make Jesus faithfully Jewish, but they can't get it right.

Vermes[169] tells us that

> The title of rabbi does not seem to have acquired in Jesus' lifetime the meaning attached to it in later ages of a fully trained exponent of Scripture and tradition.[170] None of his predecessors or contemporaries, not even the great Hillel or Shammai, or the elder Gamaliel, are referred to as rabbi in the Mishnah or the Talmud . . . [A]ll three synoptic evangelists assert at the outset of his preaching career that his style *differed* from that of the scribes. . . . The proposal advanced by the form critics that many of the scholastic debates and arguments between Jesus and the Pharisees should be postdated and identified as exchanges between the leaders of the Jerusalem church, the 'Judaizing' circles of Palestinian Christianity, and their Pharisee opponents, appears in consequence

---

169. Geza Vermes, *The Gospel of Jesus the Jew*. Riddell Memorial Lectures, Forty-eighth series (University of Newcastle upon Tyne, 1981), pp. 19, 20.

170. Was Jesus a rabbi? Several of these books admit that "rabbi" was not an "official" title until later but was an informal one already in Jesus' day, but then they proceed to describe Jesus in terms of the later model! Sigal draws a helpful terminological distinction here, tracing a similar line between, first, "proto-rabbis" like Hillel, Shammai, etc., second, the Mishnaic rabbis, to whom the term "rabbi" properly applies, and third, the Pharisees ("separatists"). These last were narrow, marginal sectarians including Qumran covenanters. Jesus, Sigal thinks, was pestered by these Pharisees, not by the proto-rabbis. Phillip Sigal, *The Halakhah of Jesus of Nazareth according to the Gospel of Matthew*. Studies in Biblical Literature Number 18 (Atlanta: Society of Biblical Literature, 2007).

very persuasive.[171]

Gentile Christians became greatly exercised about food and Sabbath laws, while these would have been much less controversial in Galilean villages in Jesus' lifetime. Very likely . . . the passages in the gospels . . . arose from the . . . disputes in Christian churches after Jesus' lifetime. . . . I regard it as almost certain that the *prominence* of Sabbath disputes and the verses on the food laws (Mark 7) reflects the situation of Christian churches after Gentiles started to be admitted to the movement.[172]

Bingo! This is the flush that sends Brad Young and his kin right down the toilet.

---

171. Vermes, *Gospel of Jesus the Jew,* pp. 19–20.

172 Vermes, *Gospel of Jesus the* Jew, p. 223.

PART TWO
THE FOUR LIVING CREATURES

5 ASCENDED ARCHANGEL

If Jesus was not the rabbi so many would like to make him, what was he? I see at least four live alternatives. I will now attempt to make the case for each one. Obviously, I do not think all four are true. My point is simply to show that any of these are plausible. You're not stuck with Rabbi Jesus. Most of these possible Jesuses will not be familiar, but that should not count against them, and I hereby urge my readers to examine their reflex reactions so as to avoid this lazy default-mentality. Finally, you may be thinking that you face a dilemma of over-choice. If a decent enough case can be made for so many Jesus models, how can the intellectually honest person find himself genuinely convinced by any one of them? This conundrum is nothing new: even conventional Jesus scholars, who entertain various Jesus hypotheses, face it all the time, and, as Pyrrho of Elis, the founder of the ancient Skeptic school of philosophy, observed, if the arguments for any competing viewpoint were really convincing, all debates would have been settled long ago. The historian knows that, ultimately, one's historical judgments must be provisional, tentative, and open to change—just like scientific "orthodoxies." Such uncertainty troubles only those who demand a dogma to which they can cling like a security blanket. But if that is you, why are you reading this book?

"We know that some Jews thought it was right to worship angels in no small part because a number of our surviving texts insist that it *not* be done. You don't get laws prohibiting activities that are never performed."[173] Bart Ehrman is responding to scholars who have denied that some Jews practiced the worship of angels in pre-Christian times. In fact there was a strong tradition of belief in the elevation of various biblical patriarchs to heavenly glory and angelic, even divine, status.

Where did this angel worship come from? First, it is important to keep in mind that angels were identified with stars, "the heavenly hosts." When Judah was vassal to the Assyrian Empire, the hosts of heaven had their own floor space in the Jerusalem Temple. The ancient Song of Deborah summoned the stars to fight on Israel's side (Judg. 5:20). Second, the Priestly creation account in the first chapter of Genesis says the celestial bodies were assigned to "rule" the night and the day. And, similarly, in the archaic poem in Deuteronomy 32, the ultimate God, El Elyon, decides how many nations to create by first counting his sons, the lesser deities, then creating enough nations so each of the godlings might rule his own fiefdom. There were, let's see, seventy sons of God, so, *voila*, seventy countries. Rimmon was assigned Syria (2 Kgs. 5:18). Persia had its own angel prince (Dan. 10:13). And Yahweh, another of the divine sons, picked Israel as his protégé. Each nation, then, properly worships its godling, *including Israel*. This means that, as in Galatians 4:19 and Colossians 28, both Israel and the Gentiles worshipped the elemental spirits (the angels presiding over weather, etc.). Thus the worship of angels (Col. 2:18).

This is perhaps why we read of "the Angel of Yahweh," i.e., the Angel Yahweh (i.e., without the "of"), the Lesser Yahweh ("My name is in him"). Yahweh, then, was at first one of the sons of Elyon. This was before the so-called Deuteronomic Reform, which demoted the sons of El to the status of mere angels and fused Elyon and Yah-

---

173. Bart D. Ehrman, *How Jesus Became God: The Exaltation of a Jewish Preacher from Galilee* (New York: HarperOne, 2014), pp. 54–55.

weh. Despite the Deuteronomic attempt to identify Yahweh with El Elyon,[174] many refused to accept the changes. Their resistance was expressed theologically and mythically. For instance, Gnostics clearly regarded Yahweh Sabaoth (whose name they garbled into "Ialdabaoth") as a self-aggrandizing godling, the god of Israel, far inferior to the ultimate deity (El Elyon) whose throne he sought to usurp. Via the traditional (re)use of the Sons of God/Daughters of men story (Gen. 6:1–4), the gods/angels of the nations became the sinister Archons ("rulers"). Since (as in Galatians 3:19) it was the angels/ Archons who gave the Law, not the Ultimate God, those who kept the Law were (unwittingly) worshipping the true authors of their religion, the angels (as were all the pagans!).

Margaret Barker argues that early Christians thought Jesus was the Old Testament Angel of Yahweh. In other words, Jesus was Yahweh, appearing on earth as he had several times in ancient Israel. When he spoke of his Father in heaven, he was referring to El Elyon. One crucial bit of evidence for this is that the New Testament never calls Jesus "the son of the Lord," i.e., the son of Yahweh. Because he *was* Yahweh! He was instead "the Son of *God*" (i.e., Elyon). Think of the so-called kenosis hymn in Philippians 2:6–11 in which the pre-existent Jesus disdains any notion of usurping equality with God. Should this not be read as a rejection of the Deuteronomic decree that one must henceforth believe Yahweh was the same as Elyon?

Some argue that Galatians 4:14 implies that Paul understood the pre-existent Christ not as God but as an angel (as did Justin Martyr and some other early Christians[175]). When it says, "You welcomed

---

174. Margaret Barker, *The Great Angel: A Study of Israel's Second God* (Louisville: Westminster / John Knox Press, 1992), chapter two, "The Evidence of the Exile," pp. 12–27.

175. Aloys Grillmeier, *Christ in the Christian Tradition: From the Apostolic Age to Chalcedon (451)*. Trans. J.W. Bowden (New York: Sheed & Ward, 1965), pp. 52–53; Jean Daniélou, *The Theology of Jewish Christianity*. The Development of Christian Doctrine Before the Council of Nicaea Volume I. Trans. John A. Baker (London: Darton, Longman & Todd / Chicago: Henry

me as an angel of God, as Jesus Christ himself," should we take it
to mean "not only as an angel, but more than that, even as Jesus
Christ himself," or rather "as an angel, and not just any angel, but
Jesus Christ in particular"? But the point is really moot in view of
Jewish angelology and the belief in the exaltation of certain biblical
patriarchs.

Bart Ehrman distinguishes between ancient Jewish beliefs in im-
mortals who temporarily became mortals on the one hand and mortals exalted to immortality on the other. The first group (e.g., Eve,
Abel, Seth,[176] Jacob, and Joseph) were earthly avatars of pre-existent
heavenly/divine beings, archangels, etc., who resumed their celestial
existence once their earthly tasks were done. Sometimes such a being was even identified as the very Angel of the Lord or even as a
"Lesser Yahweh" (a survival of the earlier ditheistic belief in Yahweh
as Elyon's Son). The second group overlapped the first and included
Adam, Abel,[177] Enoch, and Moses. These attained heavenly glory and
power as a well-deserved reward for heroism and holiness.

The whole schema no doubt stems from the ancient Sacred King
mythology.[178] In the course of the New Year festival, whether in Je-

Regnery, 1964), chapter 4, "The Trinity and Angelology," pp. 117–146; Richard N. Longenecker, *The Christology of Early Jewish Christianity*. Studies
in Biblical Theology Second Series 17 (Naperville: Alec R. Allenson, 1970),
pp. 26–31; Loren T. Stuckenbruck, *Angel Veneration and Christology: A
Study in Early Judaism and in the Christology of the Apocalypse of John*.
Wissenschaftliche Untersuchungen zum Neuen Testament 2. Reihe 70
(Tübingen: J.C.B. Mohr (Paul Siebeck, 1995), p. 138, note 238.

176. E.S. Drower, *The Secret Adam: A Study of Nasorean Gnosis* (Oxford
at the Clarendon Press, 1930), chapter IV. "Adam and his Sons," pp. 34–38.
The Apocalypse of Sethel, preserved by the Manicheans, has Seth born a
man but transformed into an angel.

177. See Phillip B. Munroe III, *Four Powers in Heaven: The Interpreta-
tion of Daniel 7 in the Testament of Abraham*. Journal for the Study of the
Pseudepigrapha Supplement Series 28 (Sheffield: Sheffield Academic
Press, 1998).

178. Geo Widengren, *The Ascension of the Apostle and the Heavenly
Book*. King and Saviour III. Uppsala Universitets Arsskrift 1950: 7 (Uppsala:

rusalem or in Babylon, the king would renew his royal mandate by ritually play-acting the primordial victory of the storm god over the Chaos Dragon, which proved his merit to become the new king of gods. This ordeal seems to have included the death and resurrection of the god as when Marduk was devoured by the dragon Tiamat but then fought his way out of the belly of the beast. The king approached the high priest, who knocked his crown off and boxed his ears, his humiliation marking his declining powers, in turn symbolizing the waning of nature due, it was believed, to the sins of the king's subjects, which iniquities their king now vicariously bore. His crown restored, the king would enter the temple where, behind closed doors, his subjects believed, he should ascend to heaven (of which the temple was the earthly effigy) and there be shown as much of the Tablets of Destiny as "precorded" the events of the coming year. The king, now briefed with the information needed to anticipate crises and deal with them wisely, would henceforth function as Yahweh's or Marduk's vicar, his counterpart on earth, wielding divine authority, even bearing divine nature. Upon taking (or re-taking) the throne, the king became God's Son and Messiah (as attested in Psalm 2, a coronation hymn). It sounds just like Enoch, Moses—and Jesus. Once the Judean monarchy was destroyed by Nebuchadnezzar, the whole schema was transferred to various biblical heroes.

Adam was an angel, though soon to be a fallen one: "I commanded my wisdom to create man.... And on the earth I assigned him to be a second angel, honored and great and glorious." (2 Enoch 30:8–11, first century CE).[179]

With the archangel Michael as guide, Abraham witnesses the following spectacle.

A.B. Lundequistska Bokhandeln, 1950), p. 33.

179. "2 (Slavonic Apocalypse of) Enoch." Trans. F.I. Andersen. In Charlesworth, ed., *Old Testament Pseudepigrapha*. Vol.1, *Apocalyptic Literature and Testaments* (Garden City: Doubleday, 1983), pp. 151–152.

So Michael turned the [cherub-borne] chariot and brought Abraham to the east, to the first gate of heaven; and Abraham saw two
ways, the one narrow and contracted, the other broad and spa-
cious, and there he saw two gates, the one broad on the broad
way, and the other narrow on the narrow way. And outside the
two gates there he saw a man sitting upon a gilded throne, and
the appearance of that man was terrible, as of the Lord. And they
saw many souls driven by angels and led in through the broad
gate, and other souls, few in number, that were taken by the angels through the narrow gate. And when the wonderful one who
sat upon the golden throne saw few entering through the narrow
gate, and many entering through the broad one, straightway that
wonderful one tore the hairs of his head and the sides of his beard,
and threw himself on the ground from his throne, weeping and
lamenting. But when he saw many souls entering through the narrow gate, then he arose from the ground and sat upon his throne
in great joy, rejoicing and exulting. And Abraham asked the chief-
captain, "My Lord chief-captain, who is this most marvelous man,
adorned with such glory, and sometimes he weeps and laments,
and sometimes he rejoices and exults?" The incorporeal one said:
"This is the first-created Adam who is in such glory, and he looks
upon the world because all are born from him, and when he sees
many souls going through the narrow gate, then he arises and sits
upon his throne rejoicing and exulting in joy, because this narrow gate is that of the just, that leads to life, and they that enter
through it go into Paradise. For this, then, the first-created Adam
rejoices, because he sees the souls being saved. But when he sees
many souls entering through the broad gate, then he pulls out the
hairs of his head, and casts himself on the ground weeping and
lamenting bitterly, for the broad gate is that of sinners, which leads
to destruction and eternal punishment. And for this the first-
formed Adam falls from his throne weeping and lamenting for the
destruction of sinners, for they are many that are lost, and they are
few that are saved, for in seven thousand there is scarcely found
one soul saved, being righteous and undefiled."

While he was yet saying these things to me, behold two angels, fiery in aspect, and pitiless in mind, and severe in look, and they drove on thousands of souls, pitilessly lashing them with fiery thongs. The angel laid hold of one soul, and they drove all the souls in at the broad gate to destruction. So we also went along with the angels, and came within that broad gate, and between the two gates stood a throne terrible of aspect, of terrible crystal, gleaming as fire, and upon it sat a wondrous man bright as the sun, like to the Son of God. Before him stood a table like crystal, all of gold and fine linen, and upon the table there was lying a book, the thickness of it six cubits, and the breadth of it ten cubits, and on the right and left of it stood two angels holding paper and ink and pen. Before the table sat an angel of light, holding in his hand a balance, and on his left sat an angel all fiery, pitiless, and severe, holding in his hand a trumpet, having within it all-consuming fire with which to try the sinners. The wondrous man who sat upon the throne himself judged and sentenced the souls, and the two angels on the right and on the left wrote down, the one on the right the righteousness and the one on the left the wickedness. The one before the table, who held the balance, weighed the souls, and the fiery angel, who held the fire, tried the souls.

And Abraham asked the chief-captain Michael, "What is this that we behold?" And the chief-captain said, "These things that you see, holy Abraham, are the judgment and recompense." And behold the angel holding the soul in his hand, and he brought it before the judge, and the judge said to one of the angels that served him, "Open me this book, and find me the sins of this soul." And opening the book he found its sins and its righteousness equally balanced, and he neither gave it to the tormentors, nor to those that were saved, but set it in the midst.

And Abraham said, "My Lord chief-captain, who is this most wondrous judge? And who are the angels that write down? And who is the angel like the sun, holding the balance? And who is the fiery angel holding the fire?" The chief-captain said, "Do you see, most holy Abraham, the terrible man sitting upon the throne?

This is the son of the first created Adam, who is called Abel, whom the wicked Cain killed, and he sits thus to judge all creation, and examines righteous men and sinners. For God has said, 'I shall not judge you, but every man born of man shall be judged.' Therefore he has given to him judgment, to judge the world until his great and glorious coming, and then, O righteous Abraham, is the perfect judgment and recompense, eternal and unchangeable, which no one can alter. For every man has come from the first-created, and therefore they are first judged here by his son, and at the second coming they shall be judged by the twelve tribes of Israel, every breath and every creature. But the third time they shall be judged by the Lord God of all, and then, indeed, the end of that judgment is near, and the sentence terrible, and there is none to deliver. And now by three tribunals the judgment of the world and the recompense is made, and for this reason a matter is not finally confirmed by one or two witnesses, but by three witnesses shall everything be established. The two angels on the right hand and on the left, these are they that write down the sins and the righteousness, the one on the right hand writes down the righteousness, and the one on the left the sins. The angel like the sun, holding the balance in his hand, is the archangel, Dokiel the just weigher, and he weighs the righteousnesses and sins with the righteousness of God. The fiery and pitiless angel, holding the fire in his hand, is the archangel Puruel, who has power over fire, and tries the works of men through fire, and if the fire consume the work of any man, the angel of judgment immediately seizes him, and carries him away to the place of sinners, a most bitter place of punishment. But if the fire approves the work of anyone, and does not seize upon it, that man is justified, and the angel of righteousness takes him and carries him up to be saved in the lot of the just. And thus, most righteous Abraham, all things in all men are tried by fire and the balance." (Testament of Abraham CE, 11–13, first century)[180]

An Uthra was called forth from the side of that Lord of Great-

---

180. Trans. W.A. Craigie http://www.newadvent.org/fathers/1007.htm.

ness and was sent out, whose name is Hibil [i.e., Abel]-Ziwa and
who is called 'Gabriel the Messenger' . . .When the sublime King
of Light willed it, he called me forth from the radiance and light in
which he stands . . . and spoke to him: 'Set off, go to the World of
Darkness. . . ' He said to him: 'Go, trample down the darkness and
the inhabitants which were fashioned from it. Solidify the earth,
span out the firmament, and make stars in it.' (Right Ginza I, first-
third century CE)[181]

Mother Eve jump-starts the torpid Adam, the mud-pie protégé
of the evil Archons, and winds up fashioning an earthly counterpart
of herself as a decoy to divert the lustful angels.

And the spirit-endowed woman came to him and spoke with him,
saying, "Arise, Adam." And when he saw her, he said, "It is you
who have given me life; you will be called 'mother of the living'.—
For it is she who is my mother. It is she who is the physician, and
the woman, and she who has given birth." Then the authorities
came up to their Adam. And when they saw his female counterpart speaking with him, they became agitated with great agita-
tion; and they became enamored of her. They said to one another,
"Come, let us sow our seed in her," and they pursued her. And she
laughed at them for their witlessness and their blindness; and in
their clutches she became a tree, and left before them her shad-
owy reflection resembling herself; and they defiled it foully.—And
they defiled the stamp of her voice, so that by the form they had
modeled, together with their (own) image, they made themselves
liable to condemnation. Then the female spiritual principle came
in the snake, the instructor; and it taught them, saying, "What did
he say to you? Was it, 'From every tree in the garden shall you eat;
yet—from the tree of recognizing good and evil do not eat'?" The

181. Trans. Peter W. Coxon. In Werner Foerster, ed., *Gnosis: A Selection
of Gnostic Texts II. Coptic and Mandean Sources.* (Oxford at the Clarendon
Press, 1974), pp. 182–183.

carnal woman said, "Not only did he say 'Do not eat', but even 'Do not touch it; for the day you eat from it, with death you are going to die.'" (Hypostasis of the Archons, third century CE)[182]

Scholars have mostly interpreted the kenosis hymn in Philippians 2:6–11 as a description of the incarnation of Jesus Christ. James D.G. Dunn,[183] for example, sees in these verses a contrast between Adam's fatal misstep of seeking equality with God ("You shall be like God.") and Jesus' disdain for such self-aggrandizement. I think this is not quite right. In my view the kenosis hymn not only *reflects* the story of Adam; it *is* the story of Adam, an alternative version analogous to that in Ezekiel 28.[184] "Being in the form of God, he did not think equality with God a thing to be seized but emptied himself, taking the form of a servant, etc." This sounds to me like an express repudiation of the Genesis version, asserting *not* that Christ refused to make the same mistake that Adam had made, but rather that *Adam* did not make the mistake some *said*[185] he made. He did indeed depart from his original heavenly state to assume the burdens of earthly existence, but this was not a punishment as some believed. Rather it was voluntary (perhaps in order "to learn obedience" as in Hebrews 5:8). Originally the text lacked the phrase "even death on a cross"[186] but referred only to death, mortality in general, the human

182. Trans. Bentley Layton. http://www.gnosis.org/naghamm/hypostas.html.

183. James D.G. Dunn, *Christology in the Making: An Inquiry into the Origins of the Doctrine of the Incarnation* (London: SCM Press, Second edition 1989), pp. xviii-xix, 113–121.

184. Cf., Margaret Barker, *The Gate of Heaven: The History and Symbolism of the Temple in Jerusalem* (London: SPCK, 1991), pp. 70–75.

185. James H. Charlesworth, "The Portrayal of the Righteous as an Angel." In George W.E. Nickelsburg and John J. Collins, eds., *Ideal Figures in Ancient Judaism: Profiles and Paradigms*. Septuagint and Cognate Studies 12 (Chico: Scholars Press, 1980), p. 138.

186. Ralph P. Martin, *Carmen Christi: Philippians ii.5–11 in Recent Interpretation and in the Setting of Early Christian Worship*. Society for New Testament Studies Monograph Series 4 (Cambridge at the University Press,

lot. God then exalted Adam to heavenly glory, the state in which we see him in the Testament of Abraham, investing him with the divine Name, "Yahweh Is Salvation." Just like Moses and Metatron and the angel Yahoel.[187] Philippians 2:6–11 obviously applies the story to "Jesus," but it is not about Jesus of Nazareth. "Jesus" ("Yahweh Is Salvation") in the hymn referred to the Great Angel receiving the divine Name, just like Yahoel and the Lesser Yahweh. I suspect this is the theo-mythical background for the Ebionites' and the Naassenes' identification of Jesus with Adam.

Enoch relates how he became transfigured into the angel Metatron:

> The Holy One, blessed be he, laid his hand on me and blessed me with 1,365,000 blessings. I was enlarged and increased in size till I matched the world in length and breadth. He made to grow on me 72 wings, 36 on one side and 36 on the other, and each single wing covered the entire world. He fixed in me 365,000 eyes and each eye was like the Great Light. . . . After all this . . . the Holy One, blessed be he, made for me a throne like the throne of glory. . . . Out of the love which he had for me, more than for all the denizens of the heights, the Holy One, blessed be he, . . . fashioned for me a kingly crown in which 49 refulgent stones were placed, each like the sun's orb. . . . He set it upon my head and he called me, "The lesser Yahweh" in the presence of his whole household in the height, as it is written, "My name is in him." (3 Enoch 9:1–4; 10:1; 12:1–5, 5ᵗʰ to 6ᵗʰ century CE)[188]

1967), pp. 220–222.

187. Barker, *Great Angel*, pp. 77, 121; Jarl E. Fossum, *The Name of God and the Angel of the Lord: Samaritan and Jewish Concepts of Intermediation and the Origin of Gnosticism.* Wissenschaftliche Untersuchungen zum Neuen Testament 36 (Tübingen: J.C.B. Mohr (Paul Siebeck), 1987), pp. 289, 318–321; Charles A. Gieschen, *Angelomorphic Christology: Antecedents and Early Evidence.* Arbeiten zur Geschichte des Antiken Judentums und des Urchristentums XLII (Leiden: Brill, 1998), pp. 142–144.

188. "3 (Hebrew Apocalypse of) Enoch." Trans. P. Alexander. In James H.

Jacob reveals his own angelic nature:

> Thus Jacob says: "I, Jacob, who speak to you, and Israel, I am an angel of God, a ruling spirit, and Abraham and Isaac were created before every work of God; and I am Jacob, called Jacob by men, but my name is Israel, called Israel by God, a man seeing God, because I am the first-born of every creature which God caused to live." And he adds: "When I was coming from Mesopotamia of Syria, Uriel, the angel of God, came forth, and said, 'I have come down to the earth and made my dwelling among men, and I am called Jacob by name.' He was angry with me and fought with me and wrestled against me, saying that his name and the name of Him who is before every angel should be before my name. And I told him his name and how great he was among the sons of God; 'Are you not Uriel my eighth, and I am Israel and archangel of the power of the Lord and a chief captain among the sons of God? Am not I Israel, the first minister in the sight of God, and I invoked my God by the inextinguishable name?'" (Prayer of Joseph, first-fourth century CE)[189]

Asenath,[190] about to become the bride of Joseph, receives a surprise visit from Joseph's angelic counterpart.

> And lo, the heaven was torn open near the morning star and an indescribable light appeared. And Aseneth fell on her face upon the ashes; and there came to her a man from heaven and stood at her head; and he called to her, "Aseneth". And she said, "Who called me? For the door of my room is shut and the tower is high: how then did anyone get into my room?" And the man called her

---

Charlesworth, ed., *The Old Testament Pseudepigrapha*. Vol. 1, pp. 263–265.

189. Quoted in Origen, *Commentary on the Gospel of John - Book II*, 25 Allan Menzies translation (1896), https://en.wikipedia.org/wiki/Prayer_of_Joseph.

190. Also spelled "Aseneth" as in the ensuing passage.

a second time and said, "Aseneth, Aseneth;" and she said, "Here am I, my lord, tell me who you are." And the man said, "I am the commander of the Lord's house and chief captain of all the host of the Most High: stand up, and I will speak to you." And she looked up and saw a man like Joseph in every respect, with a robe and a crown and a royal staff. But his face was like lightning, and his eyes were like the light of the sun, and the hairs of his head like flames of fire, and his hands and feet like iron from the fire. And Aseneth looked *at him*, and she fell on her face at his feet in great fear and trembling. And the man said to her, "Take heart, Aseneth, and do not be afraid; but stand up, and I will speak to you."[191] (Joseph and Asenath XIV: 3–23, 100–110 CE)

Both Jewish and Samaritan traditions elevated Moses the lawgiver to supramundane heights, frequently assimilating his ascent of Sinai to receive the Law to his final assumption into heaven (the latter inferred, correctly, I think, from the coy statement of Deuteronomy 34:5–6 that no one knows his burial place), understanding his elevation as to a divine deputy of Yahweh. Moses' father-in-law Jethro interprets Moses' dream-vision of his divine coronation.

> "Methought upon Mount Sinai's brow I saw
> A mighty throne that reached to heaven's high vault,
> Whereon there sat a man of noblest mien
> Wearing a royal crown; whose left hand held
> A mighty sceptre; and his right to me
> Made sign, and I stood forth before the throne.
> He gave me then the sceptre and the crown,
> And bade me sit upon the royal throne,
> From which himself removed. Thence I looked forth
> Upon the earth's wide circle, and beneath
> The earth itself, and high above the heaven.

---

191. Trans. David Cook. http://www.markgoodacre.org/aseneth/translat. htm#XIV.

Then at my feet, behold! a thousand stars
Began to fall, and I their number told,
As they passed by me like an armed host:
And I in terror started up from sleep."

Then his father-in-law thus interprets the dream:

"This sign from God bodes good to thee, my friend.
Would I might live to see thy lot fulfilled!
A mighty throne shalt thou set up, and be
Thyself the leader and the judge of men!
And as o'er all the peopled earth thine eye
Looked forth, and underneath the earth, and high
Above God's heaven; so shall thy mind survey
All things in time, past, present, and to come."
(Ezekiel the Tragedian, second century BCE)[192]

Exalted is the great prophet Moses whom his Lord vested with His name. He dwelt in the mysteries and was crowned with the light. The True One was revealed to him and gave him His handwriting; He made him drink from ten glorious fountains, seven on high and three below. (*Memar Markah* ii:12, 14th century CE)[193]

I am not sure the two categories Ehrman delineates are hermetically sealed. I think that what first looks like adoptionism or exaltation "Christology" of these patriarchs turns out to be more of an incarnational "Christology" since many of the figures are also understood by the ancients to have been pre-existent entities. Enoch was already a heavenly figure before he came to earth. He had forgotten it till informed that he himself was the ancient Son of Man seated at

---

192. Trans. E.H. Gifford http://jewishchristianlit.com/Texts/OT/EzekielThe-Tragedian.html.

193. Trans. John Macdonald in Macdonald, *The Theology of the Samaritans* New Testament Library (London: SCM Press, 1964), p. 80.

the right hand of the Ancient of Days:

> And that Head of Days came with Michael and Gabriel, Raphael and Phanuel, and thousands and ten thousands of angels without numbers. And that angel came to me, and greeted me with his voice, and said to me, 'You are the Son of Man who was born to righteousness.' (1 Enoch LXXI:13–14, first century BCE–CE).[194]

Boyarin theorizes that two rival traditions have been fused: one in which the ascended figure has been adopted unto heavenly glory and another according to which he was a preexistent angel who appeared on earth. The result was one in which the revealer was an angel but, a la kenosis, forgot his true nature/identity once appearing on earth until he ascended to heaven.[195] We find exactly this form in the Hymn of the Pearl, imbedded in the Acts of Thomas.

I.

When, a quite little child, I was dwelling
In the House of my Father's Kingdom,

And in the wealth and the glories
Of my Up-bringers I was delighting,

From the East, our Home, my Parents
Forth-sent me with journey-provision.

Indeed from the wealth of our Treasure,
They bound up for me a load.

Large was it, yet was it so light
That all alone I could bear it.

---

194. Trans. M.A. Knibb. In H.F.D. Sparks, ed., *The Apocryphal Old Testament* (Oxford: Clarendon Press, 1984), p. 256.

195 Boyarin, p. 90.

II.

Gold from the Land of Beth-Ellaya,
Silver from Gazak the Great,
Chalcedonies of India,
Iris-hued [Opals?] from Kāshan.
They girt me with Adamant [also]
That hath power to cut even iron.
My Glorious Robe they took off me
Which in their love they had wrought me,
And my Purple Mantle [also]
Which was woven to match with my stature.

III.

And with me They [then] made a compact;
In my heart wrote it, not to forget it:

"If thou goest down into Egypt,
And thence thou bring'st the one Pearl—
"[The Pearl] that lies in the Sea,
Hard by the loud-breathing Serpent—
"[Then] shalt Thou put on thy Robe
And thy Mantle that goeth upon it,
"And with thy Brother, Our Second,
Shalt thou be Heir in our Kingdom."

IV.

I left the East and went down
With two Couriers [with me];
For the way was hard and dangerous,
For I was young to tread it.
I traversed the borders of Maishan,
The mart of the Eastern merchants,
And I reached the Land of Babel,
And entered the walls of Sarbāg.

Down further I went into Egypt;
And from me parted my escorts.

V.

Straightway I went to the Serpent;
Near to his lodging I settled,
To take away my Pearl
While he should sleep and should slumber.
Lone was I there, yea, all lonely;
To my fellow-lodgers a stranger.
However I saw there a noble,
From out of the Dawn-land my kinsman,
A young man fair and well favoured,
Son of Grandees; he came and he joined me.

VI.

I made him my chosen companion,
A comrade, for sharing my wares with.
He warned me against the Egyptians,
'Gainst mixing with the unclean ones.
For I had clothed me as they were,
That they might not guess I had come
From afar to take off the Pearl,
And so rouse the Serpent against me.

VII.

But from some occasion or other
They learned I was not of their country.
With their wiles they made my acquaintance;
Yea, they gave me their victuals to eat.
I forgot that I was a King's son,
And became a slave to their king.
I forgot all concerning the Pearl

For which my Parents had sent me;
And from the weight of their victuals
I sank down into a deep sleep.

VIII.

All this that now was befalling,
My Parents perceived and were anxious.
It was then proclaimed in our Kingdom,
That all should speed to our Gate—
Kings and Chieftains of Parthia,
And of the East all the Princes.
And this is the counsel they came to:
I should not be left down in Egypt.
And for me they wrote out a Letter;
And to it each Noble his Name set:

IX.

"From Us—King of Kings, thy Father,
And thy Mother, Queen of the Dawn-land,
"And from Our Second, thy Brother—
To thee, Son, down in Egypt, Our Greeting!
"Up and arise from thy sleep,
Give ear to the words of Our Letter!
"Remember that thou art a King's son;
See whom thou hast served in thy slavedom.
Bethink thyself of the Pearl
For which thou didst journey to Egypt.

X.

"Remember thy Glorious Robe,
Thy Splendid Mantle remember,
"To put on and wear as adornment,
When thy Name may be read in the Book of the Heroes,

"And with Our Successor, thy Brother,
Thou mayest be Heir in Our Kingdom."
My Letter was [surely] a Letter
The King had sealed up with His Right Hand,
'Gainst the Children of Babel, the wicked,
The tyrannical Daimons of Sarbāg.

XI.

It flew in the form of the Eagle,
Of all the winged tribes the king-bird;
It flew and alighted beside me,
And turned into speech altogether.
At its voice and the sound of its winging,
I waked and arose from my deep sleep.
Unto me I took it and kissed it;
I loosed its seal and I read it.
E'en as it stood in my heart writ,
The words of my Letter were written.

XII.

I remembered that I was a King's son,
And my rank did long for its nature.
I bethought me again of the Pearl,
For which I was sent down to Egypt.
And I began [then] to charm him,
The terrible loud-breathing Serpent.
I lulled him to sleep and to slumber,
Chanting o'er him the Name of my Father,
The Name of our Second, [my Brother],
And [Name] of my Mother, the East-Queen.

XIII.

And [thereon] I snatched up the Pearl,

And turned to the House of my Father.
Their filthy and unclean garments
I stripped off and left in their country.
To the way that I came I betook me,
To the Light of our Home, to the Dawn-land.
On the road I found [there] before me,
My Letter that had aroused me—
As with its voice it had roused me,
So now with its light it did lead me—

XIV.

On fabric of silk, in letter of red [?],
With shining appearance before me [?],
Encouraging me with its guidance,
With its love it was drawing me onward.
I went forth; through Sarbāg I passed;
I left Babel-land on my left hand;
And I reached unto Maishan the Great,
The meeting-place of the merchants,
That lieth hard by the Sea-shore.

XV.

My Glorious Robe that I'd stripped off,
And my Mantle with which it was covered,
Down from the Heights of Hyrcania,
Thither my Parents did send me,
By the hands of their Treasure-dispensers
Who trustworthy were with it trusted.
Without my recalling its fashion,—
In the House of my Father my childhood had left it,—
At once, as soon as I saw it,
The Glory looked like my own self.

XVI.

I saw it in all of me,
And saw me all in [all of] it,—
That we were twain in distinction,
And yet again one in one likeness.
I saw, too, the Treasurers also,
Who unto me had down-brought it,
Were twain [and yet] of one likeness;
For one Sign of the King was upon them—
Who through them restored me the Glory,
The Pledge of my Kingship [?].

XVII.

The Glorious Robe all-bespangled
With sparkling splendour of colours:
With Gold and also with Beryls,
Chalcedonies, iris-hued [Opals?],
With Sards of varying colours.
To match its grandeur [?], moreover, it had been completed:
With adamantine jewels
All of its seams were off-fastened.
[Moreover] the King of Kings' Image
Was depicted entirely all o'er it;
And as with Sapphires above
Was it wrought in a motley of colour.

XVIII.

I saw that moreover all o'er it
The motions of Gnosis abounding;
I saw it further was making
Ready as though for to speak.
I heard the sound of its Music
Which it whispered as it descended [?]:

"Behold him the active in deeds!
For whom I was reared with my Father;
"I too have felt in myself
How that with his works waxed my stature."

XIX.

And [now] with its Kingly motions
Was it pouring itself out towards me,
And made haste in the hands of its Givers,
That I might [take and] receive it.
And me, too, my love urged forward
To run for to meet it, to take it.
And I stretched myself forth to receive it;
With its beauty of colour I decked me,
And my Mantle of sparkling colours
I wrapped entirely all o'er me.

XX.

I clothed me therewith, and ascended
To the Gate of Greeting and Homage.
I bowed my head and did homage
To the Glory of Him who had sent it,
Whose commands I [now] had accomplished,
And who had, too, done what He'd promised.
[And there] at the Gate of His House-sons
I mingled myself with His Princes;
For He had received me with gladness,
And I was with Him in His Kingdom;

XXI.

To whom the whole of His Servants
With sweet-sounding voices sing praises.

* * * * *

He had promised that with him to the Court
Of the King of Kings I should speed,
And taking with me my Pearl
Should with him be seen by our King.
The Hymn of Judas Thomas the Apostle,
which he spake in prison, is ended.

Ebionites,[196] Philo,[197] Mandaeans,[198] and subsequent Kabbalists[199] believed Adam had been a heavenly being, even the creative Logos of God. Abel ("Hibil-Ziwa"), Seth ("Sitil"), and Enosh ("Enosh-Uth-ra") were venerated as divine beings by the Mandaeans. Samaritans (whose ancient traditions are enshrined in later texts) identified Moses as a pre-existent being of divine light who had assisted in creation.[200] Enoch/Metatron, too, was instrumental in the creation. These figures were or had been turned into versions of "the Angel of Yahweh" endowed with the Tetragrammaton ("YHWH") which in turn was widely believed to be the Word whereby God created all things. It seems hard to deny that New Testament Christology finds its proper history-of-religions context here. Jesus was exalted to divine dignity, playing Yahweh to his Father El Elyon. Yet as such he became identified with/as the Word, the Demiurge of creation. The old puzzle pieces get reshuffled to form a clearer picture.[201]

196. Schoeps, *Jewish Christianity*, pp. 68–71.

197. Stefan Nordgaard, "Paul's Appropriation of Philo's Theory of 'Two Men' in 1 Corinthians 15.45–49." *New Testament Studies* Vol. 57, no. 3, July 2011, pp. 348–365.

198. Drower, *Secret Adam*, Ibid.

199. Gershom Scholem, *Major Trends in Jewish Mysticism*. Hilda Strook Lectures, Jewish Institute of Religion. Trans. George Lichtheim (New York: Schocken Books, 1961), Seventh Lecture: "Isaac Luria and his School," pp. 244–286.

200. Macdonald, *Theology of the Samaritans*, pp. 164–165, 179.

201. If one shrugs off the seeming connection between the exaltation of Jesus and those of Enoch, Moses, etc., is it not like the attempts of Creationist ax-grinders who discount evolution, "arguing" that the similarity between

Bart Ehrman, like Larry Hurtado, Wayne A. Meeks, and others, maintains that this model was applied to a historical figure, Jesus of Nazareth. It's possible, but let's not forget that all the others without exception were mythical, i.e., fictive characters. There never was any Adam, Eve, Abel, Seth, Enosh, Enoch, Jacob, Joseph, or Moses. In fact, it is evident that Enoch and Moses, like Samson, Esau, Isaac, Elijah, and Hercules,[202] were at first sun gods pure and simple, the sun personified. As is the rule with mythological gods, they were eventually reframed as legendary demigods who moved among men though possessing divine parentage and powers.[203] So Enoch, for example, was at first a sun god, period. His lifespan of 365 years, as we now read it, was originally the 365 days of the solar year. He rose to the zenith of the heavens as the noonday sun. He walked with God across the circuit of the heavens—as the sun. But he was then retooled as an earthly man exalted (or a god incarnated)—just like the Mythicist understanding of Jesus, a celestial entity (not incarnated but) historicized. And here we have the exaltation pattern seen in Jesus: what was originally a (sun) god, a mythic being, gets demoted to a demigod human (a legendary being), but then his original character as a divinity returns (the return of the repressed) as this human figure ascends to heaven and becomes a second god, the lesser Yahweh (who is actually, a la Barker, Yahweh himself, left over from the unification of Yahweh and Elyon).

The Sacred King mythos survived and flourished in yet another

---

life-forms is pretty much coincidence? See Robert M. Price, "The Return of the Navel: The 'Omphalos' Argument in Contemporary Creationism." In *Creation/Evolution* II (Fall 1980), pp. 26–33.

202. Ignaz Goldziher, *Mythology Among the Hebrews and its Historical Development*. Trans. Russell Martineau (New York: Cooper Square, 1967), Chapter V, "The Most Prominent Figures in Hebrew Mythology," pp. 90–197; Appendix 2 by H. Steinthal, "The Legend of Samson," pp. 392–446; Robert M. Price, *Moses and Minimalism: Form Criticism vs. Fiction in the Pentateuch* (Valley, WA: Tellectual Press, 2015), pp. 118–120.

203. Jaan Puhvel, *Comparative Mythology* (Baltimore: Johns Hopkins University Press, 1987), p. 39.

form, that of Merkavah Mysticism, a meditative practice, at least as old as the Dead Sea Scrolls (which attest it). Certain sages would concentrate, individually or as a group, on Ezekiel's vision of the throne-chariot (the Merkavah) in heaven, seeking to make their own visionary ascent, as Paul does in 2 Corinthians 12:1–10, to behold the wonders of heaven. In this they were democratizing the annual "ascension" of the ancient Jewish kings into the Temple (almost literally heaven on earth[204]) to read from the Tablets of Destiny. As the old kings mimed the battle of the god against the Chaos Dragon(s), the Merkavah mystic found himself assailed from every direction by fierce angels barring his way. The sages warned of the great danger attending the visionary quest: some had died from shock. Others had misconstrued what they saw. Still others had gone insane at the greatness of the revelations vouchsafed them.

As we have seen, Bruce Chilton depicts Jesus as having a visionary ascent to the throne-chariot at his baptism when "he saw the heavens open" (Mark 1:10), though he provides no real evidence beyond that of his imagination. Margaret Barker makes the Jordan vision equally crucial for Jesus, but unlike Chilton, Barker provides evidence that at least early Christians viewed it this way. And it is this evidence that serves to make explicit the connection of Merkavah mysticism with the Sacred King mythos. Various

> texts, both baptismal liturgies and the liturgies for Epiphany, are quite clear that the dragon was overcome in the waters of the Jordan at the moment of Jesus' baptism, fulfilling Psalm 74:13: "Thou didst break the heads of the dragon on the waters," Cyril of Jerusalem explained to his catechumens: "Since it was necessary to crush the heads of the dragon, he went down into the water to bind the strong man so that we should take authority to tread on serpents and scorpions." An Epiphany hymn attributed to Severus of Antioch says that Christ by his baptism opened the way to heaven,

---

204. Barker, *Gate of Heaven*, p. 61.

brought down the Holy Spirit and crushed the head of the evil serpent on the waters. Coptic and Ethiopian prayers to consecrate the baptismal water recall how the Lord bound the seas and sealed the deeps and shattered the heads of the dragons in the water.[205]

"Thus early Christians retained elements of the Sacred King mythology which entailed the death and resurrection of the king during his defeating Leviathan" (Boyarin).[206]

> This way of looking at things is quite opposite to a scholarly tradition that assumes that Jesus came first and that Christology was created after the fact in order to explain his amazing career. The job description . . . was there already. . . . The job description was not a put-up job tailored to fit Jesus![207]

Exactly! There was an already ancient role for a potential Messiah to fill. It was a role of divine Sonship (not necessarily purely honorific) for an Anointed One, one who died and resurrected, who atoned for the sins of his people. Then whence the familiar Messiah concept we are always told was the Jewish original? By now it ought to be obvious: it was another innovation of the Deuteronomic Reformers. In the interests of emerging monotheism, just as the lesser gods were reduced to mere angels, so the divine Messiah had to become a mortal, though a righteous one, an heir of King David—and no more. But he had been more, much more. And many Jews never forgot it, any more than they ever forgot about Leviathan, still cavorting in the Book of Revelation.

The reader may be asking what any of this has to do with "Judaizing Jesus." Much in every way! For, if this is anywhere near the

---

205. Margaret Barker *The Risen Lord: The Jesus of History as the Christ of Faith* (Philadelphia: Trinity Press International, 1997), p. 39.

206. Boyarin, pp. 47–49.

207. Boyarin, p. 73.

truth, it means that the Christian Christology is based directly on the Sacred King mythology which was pre-Judaic, that is, part and parcel of that ancient Israelite religion which the Deuteronomists replaced by Judaism proper, but which continued flowing like hidden streams far(?) underground in popular belief, coming to the surface again in Gnosticism, Philonic speculation, Merkavah Mysticism—and the New Testament. In this case the halakhic, hair-splitting proto-rabbinical Jesus must be seen as an attempt, perhaps by Christian Pharisees, to remodel Jesus in a manner reminiscent of their predecessors, the Deuteronomists. It would be a Judaizing makeover.

6 GNOSTIC REDEEMER

Have you ever wondered what it could possibly mean in Revelation 13:8 when Jesus is said to have been "slain from the foundation of the world"? Perhaps it reflects an ancient belief you never heard of: the pre-cosmic attack of the evil Archons upon the Primal Man (or Man of Light), which resulted in his stolen life-giving photons vivifying the inert mud-pie creations of the Demiurge. Thus it was a saving death, followed by the resurrection of the Man of Light, though leaving spiritual photons behind, embedded within the Gnostic illuminati. (See just below on the Gnostic redeemer myth.) This myth seems to be a variant of the Vedic Purusha cosmogony, whereby the universe was the result of the celestial self-sacrifice of the gigantic Primal Man.

HYMN XC. PURUSA.

1. A thousand heads hath Purusa, a thousand eyes, a thousand feet. On every side pervading earth he fills a space ten fingers wide.

2 This Purusa is all that yet hath been and all that is to be;
The Lord of Immortality which waxes greater still by food.

3 So mighty is his greatness; yea, greater than this is Purusa.

All creatures are one-fourth of him, three-fourths eternal life in heaven.

4 With three-fourths Purusa went up: one-fourth of him again was here. Thence he strode out to every side over what eats not and what eats.

5 From him Virāj was born; again Purusa from Virāj was born. As soon as he was born he spread eastward and westward o'er the earth.

6 When Gods prepared the sacrifice with Purusa as their offering, Its oil was spring, the holy gift was autumn; summer was the wood.

7 They balmed as victim on the grass Purusa born in earliest time. With him the Deities and all Sādhyas and Rsis sacrificed.

8 From that great general sacrifice the dripping fat was gathered up. He formed the creatures of the air, and animals both wild and tame.

9 From that great general sacrifice Rcas and Sāma-hymns were born: Therefrom were spells and charms produced; the Yajus had its birth from it.

10 From it were horses born, from it all cattle with two rows of teeth: From it were generated kine, from it the goats and sheep were born.

11 When they divided Purusa how many portions did they make? What do they call his mouth, his arms? What do they call his thighs and feet?

12 The Brahman was his mouth, of both his arms was the Rājanya made. His thighs became the Vaiśya, from his feet the Śūdra was produced.

13 The Moon was gendered from his mind, and from his eye the

Sun had birth; Indra and Agni from his mouth were born, and Vāyu from his breath.

14 Forth from his navel came mid-air, the sky was fashioned from his head, Earth from his feet, and from his ear the regions. Thus they formed the worlds.

15 Seven fencing-sticks had he, thrice seven layers of fuel were prepared, When the Gods, offering sacrifice, bound, as their victim, Purusa.

16 Gods, sacrificing, sacrificed the victim; these were the earliest holy ordinances. The Mighty Ones attained the height of heaven, there where the Sādhyas, Gods of old, are dwelling.

Much debate has ensued over the Redeemer myth of Gnosticism in recent decades. Kurt Rudolph comments:

The Gnostic doctrine of the redeemer has many ramifications and cannot be compressed without more ado into a uniform picture . . . [The] various schools and writings have different views about . . . the form of the redeemer or emissary of light. Here the super-imposing of different traditions plays a large part, especially in the texts which have been subsequently "Christianized," i.e. those in which Christ has only secondarily been given a place. . . . [Richard] Reitzenstein introduced the concept "redeemed redeemer". By this he understood the idea, which occurs above all in Manicheism, that a heavenly being (the son of God or [son] of "Man") falls into darkness and is there held captive, and can return again only after leaving behind part of his being; this part forms the soul of light scattered in the world of the body (through the creation of the world and man), and for its redemption the part that returned to the beyond descends once again as a redeemer in order to redeem ("to gather together") the rest of his nature and so restore his original totality. . . . Reitzenstein merely read it into many Gnostic traditions. However the basic idea is not alien to Gnosis; on the

contrary . . . , a whole range of statements only become compre-
hensible when we start from this, that the idea of a redeemer who
sets free the "souls", as particles of light identical with his nature,
by means of the knowledge of this identity and thereby suffers the
same fate as these souls or particles of light, actually does play a
part.[208]

Rudolph speaks of the "Christianized" Gnostic texts (e.g., the
various Sethian, Zoroastrian, and Melchizedekian documents from
Nag Hammadi).This characterization by itself does not prove a
pre-Christian date for Gnosticism. It *might* be that Christian-era
members of the still-extant pre-Christian sects redacted their old
scriptures to make them Christian-friendly. But I don't buy it. The
reluctance of some scholars (e.g. Edwin M. Yamauchi,[209] a renowned
expert on Mandaeanism and an Evangelical apologist) to see Gnosticism as pre-Christian in origin seems to me cut from the same cloth
as the futile insistence that the dying-and-rising gods of the Mystery
Religions were all post-Christian imitations. This seems unlikely
partly because Christian pseudepigraphists would be more likely
to attribute their revelations to Christian apostles (as in the case of
many Nag Hammadi works attributed to Peter, James, and Mary
Magdalene). But it makes more sense if the Apocalypse of Adam, the
Paraphrase of Shem, and the Three Stelae of Seth were the work of
Jewish writers.[210]

And though Manicheism is obviously post-Christian (3rd cen-

---

208. Kurt Rudolph, *Gnosis: The Nature and History of Gnosticism*. Trans,
P.W. Coxon. Trans. ed., R. McL. Wilson (San Francisco: Harper & Row,
1983), pp. 121–122. See also Hans Jonas, *The Gnostic Religion: The Message of the Alien God and the Beginnings of Christianity* (Boston: Beacon
Press, 1963), pp. 218–228.

209. Edwin M. Yamauchi, *Pre-Christian Gnosticism: A Survey of the Proposed Evidences* (Grand Rapids: Eerdmans, 1973).

210. Walter Schmithals somewhere makes this point. Wish I could remember where!

tury), its version of the redeemer myth clearly is based on the far more ancient Babylonian royal ideology represented in the Enuma Elish.[211] Here is a relevant excerpt. It seems that the Chaos Dragons who created the gods have become tired of the irritating hubbub generated by their offspring and have decided to send armies of deadly fiends to destroy them. Learning of this plan, the gods realize they need to resist but do not feel equal to the task. But the virile young warrior god Marduk/Bel steps forth and volunteers, his one condition being that the gods acclaim him their new king, retiring old Ea. They are only too happy to oblige! In the end, Marduk triumphs and creates the heavens and the earth from the sundered bits of the dragon queen Tiamat's carcass.

> "You are Marduk, our avenger,
> We have given you kingship over the sum of the whole universe.
> Take your seat in the assembly, let your word be exalted,
> Let your weapons not miss the mark, but may they slay your
>   enemies.
> Bel,[212] spare him who trusts in you,
> But destroy the god who set his mind on evil."
> They set a constellation in the middle
> And addressed Marduk, their son,
> "Your destiny, Bel, is superior to that of all the gods,
> Command and bring about annihilation and re-creation.
> Let the constellation disappear at your utterance,
> With a second command let the constellation reappear."
> He gave the command and the constellation disappeared,
> With a second command the constellation came into being again.
> When the gods, his fathers, saw (the effect of) his utterance,

---

211. Geo Widengren, *Mesopotamian Elements in Manichaeism*. King and Saviour II. Studies in Maitet Arsskrift 1946: 3 (Uppsala: A.B. Lundequistska Bokhandeln, 1946).

212. Another name for Marduk, obviously related to the Canaanite "Baal," who is essentially the same character.

They rejoiced and offered congratulation: "Marduk is the king!"
They added to him a mace, a throne, and a rod,
They gave him an irresistible weapon that overwhelms the foe:
(They said,) "Go, cut Tiamat's throat,
And let the winds bear up her blood to give the news."

The gods, his fathers, decreed the destiny of Bel,
And set him on the road, the way of prosperity and success.
He fashioned a bow and made it his weapon,
He set an arrow in place, put the bow string on.
He took up his club and held it in his right hand,
His bow and quiver he hung at his side.
He placed lightning before him,
And filled his body with tongues of flame.
He made a net to enmesh the entrails of Tiamat,
And stationed the four winds that no part of her escape.
The South Wind, the North Wind, the East Wind,
    the West Wind,
He put beside his net, winds given by his father, Anu.
He fashioned the Evil Wind, the Dust Storm, Tempest,
The Four-fold Wind, the Seven-fold Wind, the Chaos-spreading
    Wind, the . . . . . Wind.
He sent out the seven winds that he had fashioned,
And they took their stand behind him to harass Tiamat's entrails.
Bel took up the Storm-flood, his great weapon,
He rode the fearful chariot of the irresistible storm.
Four steeds he yoked to it and harnessed them to it,
The Destroyer, The Merciless, The Trampler, The Fleet.
Their lips were parted, their teeth bore venom,
They were strangers to weariness, trained to sweep forward.
At his right hand he stationed raging battle and strife,
On the left, conflict that overwhelms a united battle array.
He was clad in a tunic, a fearful coat of mail,
And on his head he wore an aura of terror.
Bel proceeded and set out on his way,

He set his face toward the raging Tiamat.

In his lips he held a spell,

He grasped a plant to counter poison in his hand,

Thereupon they milled around him, the gods milled around him,

The gods, his fathers, milled around him, the gods milled
     around him.

Bel drew near, surveying the maw of Tiamat,

He observed the tricks of Qingu, her spouse.

As he looked, he lost his nerve,

His determination went and he faltered.

His divine aides, who were marching at his side,

Saw the warrior, the foremost, and their vision became dim.

Tiamat cast her spell without turning her neck,

In her lips she held untruth and lies [. . .]

Bel [lifted up] the Storm-flood, his great weapon,

And with these words threw it at the raging Tiamat,

"Why are you aggressive and arrogant,

 And strive to provoke battle?

The younger generation have shouted, outraging their elders,

But you, their mother, hold pity in contempt.

Qingu you have named to be your spouse,

And you have improperly appointed him to the rank of Anuship.

Against Anšar, king of the gods, you have stirred up trouble,

And against the gods, my fathers, your trouble is established.

Deploy your troops, gird on your weapons,

You and I will take our stand and do battle."

When Tiamat heard this

She went insane and lost her reason.

Tiamat cried aloud and fiercely,

All her lower members trembled beneath her.

She was reciting an incantation, kept reciting her spell,

While the (battle-)gods were sharpening their weapons of war.

Tiamat and Marduk, the sage of the gods, came together,

Joining in strife, drawing near to battle.

Bel spread out his net and enmeshed her;

He let loose the Evil Wind, the rear guard, in her face.
Tiamat opened her mouth to swallow it,
She let the Evil Wind in so that she could not close her lips.
The fierce winds weighed down her belly,
Her inwards were distended and she opened her mouth wide.
He let fly an arrow and pierced her belly,
He tore open her entrails and slit her inwards,
He bound her and extinguished her life,
He threw down her corpse and stood on it.
After he had killed Tiamat, the leader,
Her assembly dispersed, her host scattered.
Her divine aides, who went beside her,
In trembling and fear beat a retreat.
. . . . to save their lives,
But they were completely surrounded, unable to escape.
He bound them and broke their weapons,
And they lay enmeshed, sitting in a snare,
Hiding in corners, filled with grief,
Bearing his punishment, held in a prison.
The eleven creatures who were laden with fearfulness,
The throng of devils who went as grooms at her right hand,
He put ropes upon them and bound their arms,
Together with their warfare he trampled them beneath him.
Now Qingu, who had risen to power among them,
He bound and reckoned with the Dead Gods.
He took from him the Tablet of Destinies, which was
    not properly his,
Sealed it with a seal and fastened it to his own breast.
After the warrior Marduk had bound and slain his enemies,
Had . . . . the arrogant enemy . . . ,—
Had established victory for Anšar over all his foes,
Had fulfilled the desire of Nudimmud,
He strengthened his hold on the Bound Gods,
And returned to Tiamat, whom he had bound.
Bel placed his feet on the lower parts of Tiamat

And with his merciless club smashed her skull.
He severed her arteries
And let the North wind bear up (her blood) to give the news.
His fathers saw it and were glad and exulted;
They brought gifts and presents to him.
Bel rested, surveying the corpse,
In order to divide the lump by a clever scheme.
He split her into two like a dried fish:
One half of her he set up and stretched out as the heavens.
He stretched the skin and appointed a watch
With the instruction not to let her waters escape.
He crossed over the heavens, surveyed the celestial parts,
And adjusted them to match the Apsû, Nudimmud's abode.
Bel measured the shape of the Apsû
And set up Ešarra, a replica of Ešgalla.
In Ešgalla, Ešarra which he had built, and the heavens,
He settled in their shrines Anu, Enlil, and Ea.

He fashioned heavenly stations for the great gods,
And set up constellations, the patterns of the stars.
He appointed the year, marked off divisions,
And set up three stars each for the twelve months.
After he had organized the year,
He established the heavenly station of Neberu to fix the stars'
intervals.
That none should transgress or be slothful
He fixed the heavenly stations of Enlil and Ea with it.
Gates he opened on both sides,
And put strong bolts at the left and the right.
He placed the heights (of heaven) in her (Tiamat's) belly,
He created Nannar, entrusting to him the night. [Etc.]

Geo Widengren shows that the mention of Marduk's momentary hesitation is a loose end, a vestige of an earlier version, still extant in other sources,[213] according to which Marduk was initially defeated by Tiamat, imprisoned in the netherworld, and killed—before being resurrected. This is the prototype of the Gnostic story of the Redeemed Redeemer, which in turn served as the basis, actually the first version of the gospel passion of the Christ. Here we see a myth of primordial combat eventually "updated" and historicized into our familiar gospel drama of the "historical" Jesus. Just as the death of the Man of Light, dismembered by the Archons, gave life to the formerly inert human homunculi, so did Jesus, crucified by the Archons (1 Cor. 2:6–8), bring eternal life to all who believe in him.

FROM NAASSENES TO NAZARENE?

L. Gordon Rylands[214] (whose work is sadly neglected but anticipates insights more recently set forth by John Dominic Crossan[215] and others) focuses on the pre-Christian sect of the Naassenes and their belief (shared with kindred schools of thought) in a primordial god-man, whom they (and others) called "Adamas" and "Anthropos." He was connected to mortals via the Logos, sometimes symbolized as the Jordon River defying gravity by flowing upward to heaven, functioning as the Axis Mundi[216] connecting heaven and

---

213. Widengren, *Mesopotamian Elements in Manichaeism*, p. 64. See also Sidney Smith, "The Practice of Kingship in Early Semitic Kingdoms." In S.H. Hooke, *Myth, Ritual, and Kingship: Essays on the Theory and Practice of Kingship in the Ancient Near East and in Israel* (Oxford at the Clarendon Press, 1958), pp. 40–41: "It seems quite certain from these [commentaries on ritual actions connected with the myth of Marduk] that part of Marduk's story included his imprisonment in the 'mountain' of the underworld [and . . .] that the gods rescued him by boring a hole in the door of the mountain."

214. L. Gordon Rylands, *The Beginnings of Gnostic Christianity* (London: Watts, 1940).

215. John Dominic Crossan, *The Cross That Spoke: The Origins of the Passion Narrative* (New York: Harper & Row, 1988).

216. Mircea Eliade, *The Sacred and the Profane: The Nature of Religion*. Trans. Willard R. Trask (New York: Harcourt, Brace and World), 1959), pp.

earth, like Jacob's Ladder. The Logos descending into every man and woman was (as in the New Testament and Philo) called by them the "Son of Anthropos," i.e., the Son of Man. Furthermore, the resultant spiritually reborn person was also referred to as the Son of Man. "Spirit—Adamas, as the Son of Man—then descended from above and, becoming united with the soul, strove to liberate it. He too is thus exposed to the contamination of matter and is held down and tortured in his prison of flesh. By this we must understand the discipline through suffering of the spiritual nature."[217] "This is the Christ, the Son of Man, who is fashioned from the formless Logos in all who are born."[218]

> men can be separated into two classes—the pneumatic and the psychic. In the former spirit prevails over matter and liberates the soul. In the latter the Christ is put to death ... [T]he Christ in carnal men is 'a corpse dug down into the body as if in a monument and tomb.' But a psychic man is capable of becoming pneumatic, and this conversion the Naassenes called resurrection of the dead. . . . For, they said, those who are spiritually reborn out of carnal bodies are dead men who come forth from their tombs.[219]

All this is remarkably like Immanuel Kant's understanding of Christ, regeneration, death and resurrection as set forth in his *Religion Within the Limits of Reason Alone*.[220] The "Son of God" or "Son of Man" is the ideal of humanity, but actual human beings do not meet that standard due to the conditions of worldly existence. The

---

32–36.

217. Rylands, p. 128.

218. A Naassene source quoted by Hippolytus, quoted in Rylands, p. 127.

219. Rylands, pp. 128–129.

220. Immanuel Kant, *Religion Within the Limits of Reason Alone*. Trans. Theodore M. Greene and Hoyt H. Hudson (New York: Harper & Brothers, 1960).

Incarnation refers to the embedding of this "blueprint" ideal in bodies of flesh. The redemptive sufferings of Christ stand for the anguish of the repentant sinner. Christ a symbol for *sinners*? Yes, because it is only the righteous man who repents! The really sinful one doesn't give a damn, after all. The death and resurrection of the Son speak of the repentant rebirth of the individual. The gospel story is in effect the parable of the Prodigal Son writ large. It needn't have happened to a historical Jesus.

And Rylands argues that it never did. It is, he says, quite natural to infer that this "Christology" did not begin with a historical account of miracles and a miracle worker. It is a simple matter of shaving with Occam's Razor: if the gospel story is adequately accounted for by the literalizing of a spiritual allegory, why resort to seemingly far-fetched tales of a superman performing feats beyond the abilities of ordinary mortals? Such speculations flourished especially in Alexandria and recall the Logos philosophy of Philo, a "Christian before Christ" if there ever was one. His discussions of the Logos characterize this personification of the creative Wisdom of God as the firstborn Son of God, the heavenly High Priest, the celestial Adam, etc. Philo says the divine Logos whereby God made and upholds the world ("I sustained the universe to rest firm and sure upon the mighty Logos who is my viceroy" [*On Dreams* I. 241]) is symbolized in scripture by Aaron and the high priests.

> For there are, as is evident, two temples of God: one of them this universe in which there is also as High Priest his First-born, the Divine Logos, and the other the rational soul, whose priest is the real Man: (*On Dreams* I. 215) ["God's Man, the Logos of the Eternal" (*On the Confusion of Tongues* 41. 146)]
>
> This same Logos, his Archangel, . . . both pleads with the immortal as suppliant for the afflicted mortality, and acts as the ambassador of the ruler to the subject" (*Who Is the Heir?* 205). Cf. Romans 8:34; Hebrews 4:15; 1 John 2:1–2.

Both the High Priest's vestments and the veil of the Holy of Holies, says Philo, are symbols of the physical universe, and just as the priest enters the Holy of Holies through the veil and returns through it, this symbolizes the entry of the creative Logos of God through the veil separating heaven and earth. On the one hand, the Logos *is* the veil; on the other, he clothes himself in the vestments of the material world to appear here, i.e., presumably in the creation as a whole.

> And the oldest Logos of God has put on the universe as a garment. . . . He does not tear his garments for the Logos of God is the bond of all things . . . and holds together all parts, and prevents them by its constriction from breaking apart and becoming separated. (*On Flight* 112) Cf. Colossians 1:17: "He is before all things, and in him all things hold together."

In like manner, Hebrews speaks of Christ passing through the veil of his own flesh to enter the heavenly Tabernacle where he intercedes on our behalf.

Philo speaks of the Logos as a "second God": "Nothing mortal can be made in the likeness of the Most High One and Father of the Universe, but only in that of the second God, who is his Logos . . . the head of all things" (*Questions on Exodus* 2. 117)."The heavenly Man, being the eternal archetype of mankind, is therefore the Logos, and as such the First-born Son of God." He is "neither uncreated as God nor created as you, but midway between the two extremes, a surety to both sides" (*Who Is the Heir?* 205f).

Note that in these passages we seem to have a ready-made cluster of Christological associations which may have passed over into the New Testament. But traditional biblical scholars are chary of such a conclusion. They always hasten to point out that Philo's "Christological" language is not describing a historical individual like Jesus of Nazareth, but is all allegorical and metaphorical. No kidding. This is another version of the point-missing "refutation" of the theory that the resurrection of Jesus was derived from the mythical dying and rising "corn king" gods of the Mystery Religions: those gods were not even supposed to be historical persons, whereas Jesus really lived. But of course Jesus-Mythicists realize that Attis, Baal, and the rest were symbols of the annual death and return of vegetation. Their contention is that these myths have been historicized in the case of Jesus, not that Jesus was believed by Christians to be a mere symbol. Samuel Sandmel[221] remarks:

> Was the Logos a sheer, utter reality to Greek Jews, like a line on a piece of paper, or was it a mental construction [like the idea of division for which the pencil line stands], like abstract beauty? . . . Greek Jews, at the minimum, often treat the Logos as a mere abstraction; they avoid attributing to it any location in space and time; hence they ordinarily approach it on a theoretical basis, as a philosophical construct. [On the other hand,] the Logos in Christian thought was not a mere abstraction as it may have been to Philo, especially since the main lines of the Christian tradition held that Jesus lived a particular time and particular age.

James D.G. Dunn interprets Philo as intending merely that

> the Logos is what is knowable about God; the Logos is God insofar as he may be apprehended and experienced. This does not mean that we should think of the Logos, and the powers [angels], as gradations of the divine being. . . . Philo is much too Jewish for that. We should think rather of gradations of manifestations of him who alone is God.[222]

I'm sorry, but it looks to me as if Dunn is simply treating these texts as fodder for systematic theology—his own, not Philo's! He is

221. Samuel Sandmel, *We Jews and Jesus* (New York: Oxford University Press, 1965), p. 40–41.

222. Dunn, *Christology in the Making*, p. 226.

slanting the texts in the direction of strict monotheism. What *must* Philo have meant if we are to save our monotheistic stereotype of ancient Judaism? Also, as Margaret Barker says, we seem to see here an accommodation to Jewish apologetics which try to read Tannaitic orthodoxy back into an earlier spirit. Is this more "ecumenical correctness"? ("Let's let Jewish exegetes tell us what the Old Testament means.") Or is it an apologetical alliance, since Christian apologists also want an earlier monotheism to have obtained?

Larry Hurtado[223] echoes Dunn when he says

> The personification of God's attributes is of course often vivid, and, especially in the case of Wisdom, mythic imagery from the surrounding religious world is employed. Such language would seem to justify the conclusion of some scholars that divine attributes such as Wisdom were seen as actual beings in God's service, if the language is taken literally. I am persuaded, however, that this conclusion is a misunderstanding of this particular type of ancient Jewish religious language.

Hurtado is allegorizing Philo! He takes Philo's straightforward explanations of what Philo took to be allegories and treats them as if they were themselves allegorical ciphers. If one takes this approach, where does one stop? Philo identifies Moses and the Patriarchs as the Logos incarnate. If this is allegory, why isn't it with Jesus? Why assume that John's gospel meant to have Jesus literally be the incarnation of a heavenly being either?

What accounts for the apologists' urgency to build a wall between Philo's Logos and that of John, Paul, and the writer to the Hebrews? That is not difficult to fathom: they fear that someone might get the heretical idea that somewhere along the line someone started to imagine that Philo's Logos myth was history. That would be too

---

223. Larry Hurtado, *One God, One Lord: Early Christian Devotion and Ancient Jewish Monotheism* (Philadelphia: Fortress Press, 1988), p. 46.

much like Christianity, implying that the revealed gospel was no revelation but only a moment in the evolution of an extant philosophy. Some scholars[224] have posited that Christianity was actually born in Alexandria, only subsequently spreading to Jerusalem. And this would have been the occasion for historicizing, via Judaizing, Jesus to commence.

---

224. Frank R. Zindler, *The Jesus the Jews Never Knew: Sepher Toldoth Yeshu and the Quest of the Historical Jesus in Jewish Sources* (Cranford: American Atheist Press, 2003), p. 13.

ל CYNICAL SAGE

Even in antiquity no one was quite sure who started the post-Socratic Cynic philosophy in the early fourth century B.C.E: was it Antisthenes of Athens or the more famous Diogenes of Sinope? And what did the name mean? Well, Antisthenes is known to have taught in the Cynosarges building in Athens, and philosophical groups were often named for the place they used to gather. But then Diogenes famously called himself a "dog" (*kynos*), taking as his ideal the independent lifestyle of the stray mutt. Antisthenes had been a friend of Socrates and may have started the Cynic movement.

The principles of Diogenes, and of Cynicism, included, first of all, *self-sufficiency*. One ought to declare independence of all worldly realities so that you will neither need them nor care about them. Their lack will not hurt you; their loss will not sadden you. Second, *asceticism*: if you are really self-sufficient, you should put your money where your mouth is! Renounce your possessions! Diogenes himself did this, going naked and living in a barrel or a wooden tub. At first he carried a wooden drinking bowl but burned it after noticing a boy drinking water from his cupped hands. Asceticism usually denotes rigid self-deprivation of food, sleep, company, even bathing. But there were also libertine Cynics who disdained "customary" discipline and manners. Third, *shamelessness*: you must regard all social decorum, rank, custom as a mere sham, just play-acting, and thus irrelevant. All "conventions" (as the very word suggests) are unnatural, artificial; thus shamelessness is an attempt to live according to unvarnished nature. Have no respect for social conventions! *Show* no respect for them either! Alexander the Great once visited Diogenes. He was impressed with the latter's austerities and offered to grant him any request he might make. To this Diogenes replied, "Then step out of my way—you're blocking my sunlight." Alexander cried out, "If I were not Alexander, I would be Diogenes!"

Fourth, Cynics esteemed *boldness of speech*. It is only a fear of what others will think that stops us from speaking our mind. Diogenes didn't let this stop *him*! Cynics followed his example and were great street preachers. Fifth, they practiced *freedom*: the Cynic must cast away from himself the entangling restrictions of human society. Think of the things you are forced to do because they are expected of you, like attending weddings of your wife's friends. No way! Cynics took their freedom to include free love and a community of wives and goods. Some even felt free to copulate and masturbate in public! One might view the Hippies of the 1960s as a spontaneous revival of ancient Cynicism.

Finally, sixth, they affirmed *the inability of hardship to affect the wise man,* and inner freedom from outer circumstances because *everything but virtue is indifferent.* All happenings are indifferent and irrelevant except as occasions to act or *re*act in a virtuous way. They possess no other value and are not to be loved or feared on any other grounds. *Virtue is living in accordance with Nature by reason.* This means rejecting unnatural conventions and acquiescing in whatever happens to you.

Since ethics were all that mattered to the Cynics, they disdained logic, philosophy, and physics, frequently the stock in trade of philosophers, as being without moral value. They constitute what the Buddha called "questions not tending unto edification." But Cynics did believe in free will: no event or offender can force you not to act virtuously. None is capable of *making* you sad or angry. It is up to *you* to decide how you will react. They also believed that virtue is obtainable in principle and in fact. And there is no one who is unable to attain it if they wish.

Jesus was sometimes represented by early Christian artists as wearing the distinctive garb of the Cynic philosophers (whose sayings are often reflected in Q). Lucian of Samosata (a second-century CE Syrian philosopher and humorist) wrote a lampoon of one Proteus Peregrinus whom he said had first been a Cynic, then a Christian, apparently a smooth transition. In this context Lucian calls Jesus "the crucified sophist." Was he? Several scholars, notably Burton L. Mack,[225] John Dominic Crossan,[226] and David Seeley,[227] have argued the case that the historical Jesus was a Cynic preacher, either actually or virtually, whether or not he would have accepted the label.

Jesus is said to have lived in Galilee, a marginally Jewish territory which had been heavily Hellenized. Nazareth was in the middle of a dozen Greek cities. If Jesus had *not* been familiar with Greek popular philosophy it would be a surprise. We know of a handful of Cynic apostles (wandering soap-box preachers) who criss-crossed Palestine in the first centuries BCE and CE. Thus it should come as no surprise when we compare the Q sayings with the proverbs and pronouncements of the Cynics and discover striking parallels between them. Many of the sayings from both sources advise us to throw off the burdens of social respectability, family entanglements and soul-killing mundane work. Do the birds and flowers bother with such trifles? Aren't you supposed to be smarter than them? Well, then, what are you waiting for?

Jesus is depicted in the gospels as a wanderer with no place to

---

225. Mack, pp. 67–69, 73–74.

226. John Dominic Crossan, *The Historical Jesus: The Life of a Mediterranean Jewish Peasant* (San Francisco: HarperOne, 1993), chapter 4, "Poverty and Freedom," pp. 72–88.

227. David Seeley, "Jesus and the Cynics Revisited." In *Journal of Biblical Literature*. Vol. 116, no. 4, 1997, pp. 704–712.

rest his head two times in a row. Perhaps this was the way the historical Jesus lived, perhaps not. But this is the way certain of his latter-day followers lived. Did they imitate Jesus who himself was like the Cynic itinerants? Or did they get the idea directly from the Cynics themselves, and then reimagine Jesus in their own image? It wouldn't be the first time, but who knows? The Cynics wandered the roads with only a bare minimum: a cloak, a bag, a staff, precisely the list presupposed in the Mission Charge texts (Matthew 10:5–15; Mark 6:7–11; Luke 9:1–5) which stem from this group. Cynic and Christian itinerants both claimed that God had sent them to demonstrate to others the Spartan freedom of the kingdom of God (or "the government of Zeus"). They aimed cynical barbs at traditional religion (like Mark 7:18–19—why bother with food purity laws when it's all going to end up in the toilet anyway?). But they also blessed those who maltreated them.

Burton Mack believes that the earliest version/stratum of the Q document falls naturally into seven topics, all of which have a distinctly Cynic flavor. Here are the Q1 sayings, each followed by a selection of sayings by ancient Cynics which parallel them or at least show similar priorities.

Jesus said: "Blessed are the poor, for theirs is the kingdom of God." **Seneca** said: "Only the person who has despised wealth is worthy of God." **Epictetus** said: "We should not get rid of poverty, but only our opinion of it. Then we shall have plenty."

Jesus said: "Blessed are those who hunger, for they shall be filled." **Dio** said: "People used to see Diogenes shivering out in the open, often going thirsty." And "Herakles cared nothing about heat or cold, and had no use for a mattress or a wooly cape or a rug. Dressed in a dirty animal skin, living hungry, he helped the good and punished the wicked."

Jesus said: "Blessed are those who weep, for they shall laugh."
Pseudo-Heraclitus said: "So you want to know why I never laugh? It's not because I hate people, but because I detest their wickedness. . . . You are astonished because I don't laugh, but I'm astonished at those who do, happy in their wrong-doing when they ought to be dejected at failing to do what's right."

Jesus said: "I say to you, love your enemies. Bless those who curse you. Pray for those who mistreat you." **Epictetus** said: "A rather nice part of being a Cynic comes when you have to be beaten like an ass, and throughout the beating you have to love those who are beating you as though you were father or brother to them." **Diogenes** said: "How shall I defend myself against my enemy? By being good and kind towards him." **Seneca** said: "Someone gets angry with you. Challenge him with kindness in return. Enmity immediately tumbles away when one side lets it fall."

Jesus said: "If someone slaps you on the cheek, offer him the other also. If someone seizes your cloak, offer him your tunic as well." "**Musonius Rufus** said he would never indict anyone who'd injured him, nor would he advise anyone else to, not anyone who wanted to be a proper philosopher. . . . Well, if a philosopher cannot despise a slap or abuse, what use is he? . . . People sin against you. You take it without going wild, without harming the offenders. Instead you give them cause for hope of better things." **Epictetus** said: "If you're inclined to be quick-tempered, practice being abused, refusing to get cross at insults. You'll be able to go on from that to taking a slap and saying to yourself, I seem to have got entangled with a statue."

Jesus said: "Give to anyone who asks of you, and if someone seizes your belongings, do not seek them back." **Epictetus** said: "If there is a requisition and a soldier seizes {your donkey}, let it go. Do not resist or complain; otherwise you will be first beaten, and lose the donkey after all." **Pseudo-Crates** said: "Don't get cross when wise people ask you for a tribol, for it's not yours, it's theirs, and you're giving it back to them. . . . For everything belongs to God, friends have everything in common, and the wise are the friends of God." "**Diogenes** used to say we should hold out our hands to our friends palm open, not tight-fisted." **Dio** said: "What we have now is enough for us, but you take whatever you want of it."

Jesus said: "Treat others as you would have them treat you." **Seneca** said: "Take care not to harm others, so others won't harm you." **Dio** said: "Let each one here reflect how he feels towards those who try to do him down. That way he'll have a fair idea of how others must feel about him, if that's how he behaves."

Jesus said: "If you love those who love you, what credit is that to you? Do not even tax-collectors love those who love them? If you greet only your brothers, what more are you doing than others? Does not everyone do likewise? If you lend only to those you expect to pay you back, what credit is that to you? Even evil-doers lend to their fellows expecting to be repaid." **Dio** said: "I never did a kindness to win a testimonial or to gain gratitude or any favor in return." And ". . . as though it were the done thing to be stingy and tight-fisted with impoverished strangers, but to be generously welcoming with hospitable gifts only to the wealthy, from whom you clearly expected much the same in return."

Jesus said: "No, love your enemies, do good, and lend without expecting repayment. Your reward will be great, and you will be children of God. For he makes the sun rise on the evil and the good; he sends rain on the unjust and the just alike." **Musonius** said: "By and large only humankind among living creatures is an image of God. . . . As God is . . . high-minded, beneficent and humane (that's how we conceive him to be), so we must think of human beings as his image, so long as they live according to nature, and are eager to [do so]." "**Diogenes** said good men were images of the gods." **Dio** said: "The whole human race is held in high regard—and equally high regard—by God who gave it birth."

Jesus said: "Be merciful even as your Father is merciful. Judge not, lest you, too, be judged. For you will be judged by the standard you apply." "Someone asked how he could master himself. **Diogenes** replied, 'By rigorously reproaching yourself with what you reproach others with.'"

Jesus said: "Can a blind man lead a blind man? Will they not both fall into a pit?" **Philo** said: "Some people prefer to be provided with a blind guide rather than a sighted one. They're bound to take a tumble." **Dio** said: "You can no more have a fool as king than a blind man to lead you along the road."

Jesus said: "A student is not better than his teacher. It is sufficient that he should be like his teacher." "When **Diogenes** saw a boy eating a savory snack, he rightly slapped the slave looking after him; for the fault lay with the one who'd failed to teach rather than with the one who hadn't learned."

Jesus said: "How can you look at the splinter in your brother's eye while there is a two-by-four in your own eye? How can you say to your brother, 'Let me remove the splinter from your eye,' when you are not aware of the two-by-four in your own eye? Hypocrite! First take the two-by-four out of your own eye, and then you will be able to see to remove the splinter in your brother's eye." **Seneca** said: "And you, are you at liberty to examine others' wickednesses, and pass judgment on anyone . . . ? It's like someone covered in foul scabs laughing at the odd mole or wart on someone of real beauty." **Pseudo-Diogenes** said: "When the Athenians do philosophy in your way they are like people promising to heal others of ills they've not managed to cure in themselves."

Jesus said: "A good tree does not bear bad fruit. A bad tree does not bear good fruit. Do they gather figs from thistles, or thistles from figs? Every kind of tree is recognized by its fruit." **Seneca** said: "Who would think to be surprised at finding no apples on the brambles in the wood? Or be astonished because thorns and briars are not covered in useful fruits?"

Jesus said: "The good man brings forth good things from his treasury; the evil man evil things. For the mouth speaks from what fills the heart." **Seneca** said: "Evil no more gives birth to good than an olive produces figs."

Jesus said: "Why do you call me, 'Lord, lord,' and not do what I say? Everyone who hears my words and does them is like a man who built his house on a rock. The rain fell, the flood broke against the house, and it did not fall, for it had a solid foundation. But everyone who hears my words and does not do them is like a man who built his house on sand. The rain fell, the flood broke against it, and it fell, and it was a total ruin." "**Diogenes** described himself as a hound of the kind much praised, but which none of his admirers dared to take out hunting." "It was mostly people from a distance away who came to talk with **Diogenes** . . . the common motive was just to have heard him speak for a little while, so as to have something to tell other people about . . . rather than look for some improvement for themselves." "**Seneca** said: 'If you are in good health and think yourself at last fit to be your own man, I am pleased. The distinction will be mine if I can pull you away from where you are floundering in the waves. But, my dear Lucilius, I'm begging you as well as exhorting you to put down philosophical foundations deep in your heart. Then test your progress! But not by words that you speak or write. To see what strength of mind you have gained, and what unruly desires you've shed, you must test your words by your deeds.'"

"A man said to him, 'I will follow you wherever you go.' **Jesus** said to him, 'Foxes have holes, and birds of the air have nests, but the sons of men have no place to lay their heads [for the night].'" "According to Theophrastus, **Diogenes** had watched a mouse running around, not bothering to find anywhere for its nest, not worrying about the dark, showing no particular desire for things one might suppose particularly enjoyable. It was through watching this mouse that he discovered the way to cope with circumstances." "**Diogenes Laertius** said: 'No city, no house, no fatherland, a wandering beggar, living a day at a time.'" **Pseudo-Anarcharsis** said: "The whole earth is my bed." **Epictetus** said: "I've no property, no house, no wife or children, not even a straw mattress, or a shirt, or a cooking pot." **Dio** said: "I have traveled around for so long, not only without hearth or home, but without even a single attendant to take around with me."

"Another man said to him, 'First let me go and bury my father,' **Jesus** said to him, 'Let the dead bury their dead.'" **Pseudo-Crates** said: "Though the mass of people want the same result as the Cynics, once they see how difficult the way is, they steer well clear of those who propose it." "Diogenes Laertius said: 'Someone wanted to do philosophy with **Diogenes**. Diogenes gave him a tunny fish to carry around and told him to follow him. For shame the would-be disciple threw it down and left. Some time later Diogenes met him. 'Our friendship was broken up by a tunny fish,' he said with a laugh." And "Someone said to **Diogenes**, 'I'm yours to command.' He took him along and gave him a half-obol's worth of cheese to carry. He refused. 'Our friendship's been shattered,' said Diogenes, 'by a piece of cheese costing all of a half-obol.'" **Epictetus** said: "'It's not how you think it is. . . . You say, "I wear an old cloak already—I'll go on doing that. I sleep on a hard bed now, and I shall still. I'll get myself a satchel and staff, and I'll wander around, begging from the people I meet...." If you think that's how it is, stay well clear of the whole business; there's nothing in it for you,' said **Diogenes**." **Cicero** said: "If you die without a servant to wait on you, who will take you away to bury you? 'Whoever wants the house,' said **Diogenes**." **Cicero** said: "**Diogenes** was harsher ... In Cynic style he spoke more crudely, giving orders that he was to be thrown out without burial. His friends asked, 'For the birds and wild animals?' 'Certainly not! You're to put a staff near me to drive them off with.' 'How could you?' they asked. 'You'll be past all feeling.' 'Well, what harm is there in being torn to pieces by wild beasts if I'm past all feeling?'" **Lucian** said: "A little while before **Demonax** died someone asked, 'What instructions have you given about your burial?' 'No need to fuss,' he said. 'The stink will get me buried.'" **Pseudo-Diogenes** said: "There's no need to thank your parents, either for your birth, or for being the sort of person you are."

Musonius said: "Obeying your father, you're obeying the will of a fellow human being. Doing philosophy, you're obeying Zeus."

Epictetus said: "If you're not accomplishing anything, there was not much point [in] your coming in the first place. Go back and look after things at home ... you'll have a bit more pocket money, and you'll look after your father in his old age."

Jesus said: "The harvest is abundant, but the laborers are few; therefore, beg the master of the harvest to send out more laborers into the harvest." **Dio** said: "The problem may well lie with the so-called philosophers. Some of them refuse point-blank to face crowds, just won't make the effort. Perhaps they've given up hope of improving the masses." **Epictetus** said: "A true Cynic will not rest satisfied with having been well-trained himself. He must realize he's been sent as God's messenger to his fellow humans to show them where they are going astray over what is right and what is wrong."

Jesus said: "See, I send you out as lambs amid wolves." "**Crates** said that people living with flatterers were in as bad a way as calves amid wolves."

Jesus said: "Do not carry money, or a pouch, or sandals, or a staff." **Diogenes Laertius** said: "According to Diocles, **Antisthenes** was the first to double his cloak, and use just that, and carry a staff and a satchel." And "According to some, **Diogenes** was the first person to double his threadbare cloak, because he had to use it to sleep in, and he carried a satchel for his bread . . . but he took to carrying a staff for support only when he became infirm." **Pseudo-Diogenes** said: "When I'd chosen in favor of this Cynic way, Antisthenes took off the shirt and cloak I was wearing, put a doubled threadbare on me instead, slung a satchel on my shoulder, with some bread and other scraps of food, and put in a cup and a bowl. On the outside of the satchel he hung an oil flask and a scraper, and then, finally, he gave me a staff, too." **Musonius** said: "Wearing ever only one shirt is better than needing two, and wearing just a cloak with no shirt at all is better still. Going bare-foot, if you can, is better than wearing sandals." **Lucian** said: "By now **Peregrinus** had taken to long hair and a dirty threadbare cloak and a satchel, with a staff in his hand."

Jesus said: "And do not greet anyone on the road." **Lucian** said: "Seek out the most crowded places, and when you're there, keep to yourself, quite unsociable, exchanging greetings with no one, neither friend nor stranger."

Jesus said: "Whatever house you enter, say, 'Peace be to this house!' And if a man of peace is there, your protection will rest upon him. But if not, let your blessing return to you." **Diogenes**

Laertius said: "A good daemon {spirit} has come to stay in my house." {Diogenes' host speaking of his arrival}. **Pseudo-Diogenes** said: "'Is it really necessary to have something written over your doorway?' 'Yes, it is.' 'Then how about this? "Poverty lives here, evil is debarred."'" **Pseudo-Crates** said: "Don't beg your necessities from everyone, and don't accept unsolicited gifts from just anyone, either. It's not right for moral virtue to be fed by wickedness. Ask and accept only from people who've accepted an invitation into philosophy themselves."

Jesus said: "And remain in the same house, eating and drinking whatever they provide, for the laborer is worthy of his wages." **Pseudo-Dionysus** said: "You're not asking for a free gift, still less for some worse bargain, but for a contribution to the well-being of everyone . . . you are able to give back something very much better than what you got." **Epictetus** said: "A good soldier is never without someone to reward his efforts, nor is a laborer or a cobbler. Do you think it's any different for a good human being? Do you think God cares so little for the servants and witnesses he's had so much success with?"

Jesus said: "Do not go from house to house." **Epictetus** said: "It looks to me as though what you really want is to go into someone's house and stuff yourself with food."

Jesus said: "If you enter a town and they receive you, eat what they set before you. Heal the sick and say to them, 'The Kingdom of God has come near to you.'" **Epictetus** said: "A Cynic's friend must share the Cynic's scepter and his royal rule and be a worthy servant." **Demetrius** said: "Let me enjoy the wealth that is really mine. I have experienced the great and the invincible kingdom of wisdom." **Dio** said: "It is Zeus who first and foremost knows how to rule—and shares his knowledge with whom he will."

Jesus said: "But if you enter a town and they do not receive you, as you leave, shake the very dust from your feet and pronounce against them, 'Nevertheless, know this: the Kingdom of God has come near you.'" **Pseudo-Diogenes** said: "Diogenes the Cynic to you so-called Hellenes, Be damned to you . . . you lay claim to everything, but you actually know nothing." **Dio** said: "To some **Diogenes** seemed quite mad; lots despised him as a powerless good-for-nothing. Some abused him and tried insulting him by throwing bones at his feet as you do to dogs. Others, again, would come up and pull at his cloak. . . . Yet Diogenes was really like a reigning monarch walking in beggar's rags among his slaves and servants."

Jesus said: "When you pray, say: 'Father, may your name be kept in reverence. May your kingdom come. Give us today our daily bread. Cancel our debts, for we cancel the debts owed us. And do not bring us to the test." **Epictetus** said: "For everyone and for ever and always there is the father who cares for them. Why, to Odysseus, it was no hearsay matter, that Zeus is the Father of humankind, for he always thought of him as Father, and addressed him as Father, and did everything he did with him in mind." **Dio** said: "Some people do not hesitate to address {Zeus} as Father in their prayers." And "God . . . who gives us what we need to live, and life itself, and everything good, the common Father and savior and guardian of human kind . . . is addressed as King because he rules in power, and as Father, I take it, because of his care and gentleness." **Epictetus** said: "Another takes care to provide us with food." And "With peace proclaimed by God through reason . . . now no evil can befall me."

Jesus said: "Ask and it shall be given you. Seek and you shall find. Knock, and the door shall be opened to you. For every one who asks receives, and the one who seeks finds, and the door is opened to the one who knocks." **Epictetus** said: "Seek and you will find."

Jesus said: "Which of you fathers, if his son asks for bread, will give him a stone, or if he asks for a fish, will give him a snake? Therefore, if you, being evil, know how to give good gifts to your children, how much more will the Father in heaven give good things to those who ask him!" **Seneca** said: "And our parent has put close to hand whatever is going to be to our good." **Pseudo-Heraclitus** said: "People blame the gods because they don't make them rich with lots of nice things—but they don't blame their own disposition to stupidity. They must be blind to refuse the really good gifts the daimon gives."

Jesus said: "Nothing is hidden that will not one day be made known, or secret that will not eventually come to light." **Epictetus** said: "The Cynic . . . ought to have nothing of his own that he wants to hide. Otherwise . . . he's started to be afraid about externals, he's begun to feel the need for concealment. And he couldn't possibly keep anything concealed even if he wanted to. Where or how could he possibly hide himself?"

Jesus said: "What I tell you in the dark, speak in the light. And what you hear whispered in your ear, shout it from the housetops." **Pseudo-Heraclitus** said: "I shall remain as long as there are cities and inhabited countries, my learning assuring that I never fall silent." **Diogenes Laertius** said: "**Diogenes** lit a lamp in broad daylight and went around with it, saying 'I'm looking for an honest man.'"

Jesus said: "Do not fear those who can kill the body, but cannot kill the soul." **Pseudo-Diogenes** said: "Free under Father Zeus and afraid of none of the great lords." **Epictetus** said: "What tyrant or thief or court can frighten anyone who does not care about his body or its possessions?"

Jesus said: "Are not five sparrows sold at market for two cents? Yet not a single one of them falling to the ground escapes God's watchful eye. The very hairs of your head each has its number. Therefore, do not fear. You are worth more than many sparrows."

Jesus said: "Therefore I tell you, have no anxiety over your life, what you will eat, or about your body, what you shall wear. Consider the ravens. They neither sow nor reap nor gather into barns, and God feeds them. Are you not worth more than the birds? Which of you can add a single hour to your life by worrying about clothing? Consider the lilies of the field, how they grow. They neither toil nor spin: yet I tell you Solomon in all his finery was not arrayed as one of these! If God clothes the grass of the field in this manner, though it is in the field today, only to be thrown into a furnace tomorrow, will he not clothe you, you of little faith?" **Pseudo-Dionysus** said: "Hunger, cold, contempt? Poverty doesn't necessitate any of these. Not hunger, for lots of things grow from the earth and can satisfy hunger; for the dumb beasts go without clothes and don't feel it." **Musonius** said: "Good God, that's all very well, but I'm a poor man without property. Suppose I have lots of children, where am I going to get food for them all?" "Well where do the little birds go to get food to feed their young, though they're much worse off than you are—the swallows and nightingales and larks and blackbirds. . . ? Do they store away food in safe-keeping?" **Dio** said: "Why not consider the beasts and the birds, and see how much more painlessly they live than humans do, how much more pleasantly and healthfully. They are stronger, each lives the longest possible span for their kind—despite lacking hands or human intelligence. . . . They have one enormous advantage to counter-balance any ills they may suffer—they are free of property."

Jesus said: "Therefore I tell you, do not worry, saying to your-selves, 'What shall we eat?' or 'What shall we drink?' or 'What shall we wear?' For the nations do that, and your Father knows you need these things. Instead, seek his kingdom and all these things will be provided as a matter of course." **Pseudo-Anar-charsis** said: "Since I keep my time clear of the things others busy themselves with, come to me, if you need anything I have to offer. I'll refund you generously for all the gifts you current-ly take so much pleasure in." **Epictetus** said: "What's going to become of me? Is it impossible to find a traveling companion {through life} who's strong and totally reliable?' Then you think to yourself, 'If I commit myself to God, I'll make the journey in safety.'" **Epictetus** said: "We make a fuss about our little bodies, about our piffling property, about what Caesar thinks of us. And about what's going on inside us? Not a thought!" **Seneca** said: "The philosophic wise man . . . without being concerned or anx-ious about more than the bare necessities, will give his stomach and back what's due to them. Care-free and happy, he'll laugh at people busy with their riches, and at others scurrying around trying to get rich, and he'll say, 'Why postpone being yourself into the distant future?'"

Jesus said: "Sell your possessions and give {the proceeds} to the poor." **Diogenes Laertius** said: "**Crates** sold up all his proper-ty—he was from a prominent family—and realized about two hundred talents. This he shared among his fellow citizens." **Pseu-do-Diogenes** said: "I gather that you brought all your wealth to the civic assembly and handed it over to your native city. Then, standing in the middle, you shouted out, 'Crates, son of Crates, sets Crates free!'"

Jesus said: "Do not store up for yourselves treasures on earth, where moth and rust corrupt and thieves break in and steal. But store up for yourselves treasure in heaven, where moths and rust do not corrupt and thieves do not break in and steal. For where your treasure is, your heart will be there also." **Seneca** said: "Our soul knows, I tell you, that wealth does not lie where it can be heaped together. It is the soul itself that we ought to fill, not our money-chest. It is the soul that we may set above all other things, and put, god-like, in possession of the universe ... when it has taken itself off to the great heights of heaven." And "Someone who is eager for riches is also fearful for them. But no one stops to enjoy such a worrying gain; they're always at pains to add something more." **Epictetus** said: "Where the 'I' and the 'mine' are, that's the direction in which the living being is bound to incline. If they're in the flesh, that's going to dominate; if they're in one's moral choice, that's dominant."

Jesus said: "What is the kingdom of God like? To what can one compare it?" **Dio** said: "{Phidias the sculptor claims he has tried to represent something of the accepted character of God} to the extent that a mortal man can understand and represent the inconceivable nature of God."

Jesus said: "It is like a grain of mustard seed which a man took and sowed in his garden. It grew and became a tree, and the birds of the air made nests in its branches." **Seneca** said: "These words should be scattered like seeds. However small a seed is, once it's sown in suitable ground, its potential unfolds, and from something tiny it spreads out to its maximum size ... I'd say brief precepts and seeds have much in common. Great results come from small beginnings."

Jesus said: "Once a man gave a great banquet and invited many. When time came for the banquet he sent his slave to say to those who had been invited, 'Come, for everything is now ready.' But they all alike began to make excuses. The first said to him, 'I have bought a farm, and I must go and look it over. Please have me excused.' Another said, 'I have bought five yoke of oxen, and I need to inspect them. Please have me excused.' Another said, 'I have just married a wife, and I cannot come.' The slave came and reported this to his master. Then the owner said in anger, 'Go out quickly into the streets of the town and bring in as many people as you find.' And the slave went out into the streets and brought in everyone he could find, till the house was filled with guests." **Epictetus** said: "We've no end of excuses ready for our base behavior—it's our children, . . ."

Jesus said: "He who does not hate his father and mother cannot be my disciple. He who does not hate his son and daughter cannot be my disciple." **Epictetus** said: "If you'd seized his property, **Diogenes** would have let it go rather than follow you for it. If you'd seized hold of his leg, he'd have let that go—and his . . . body, his family, his friends, his native land."

Jesus said: "He who does not carry his cross and follow me cannot be my disciple." **Epictetus** said: "If you want to be crucified, just wait. The cross will come. If it seems reasonable to comply, and the circumstances are right, then it's to be carried through, and your integrity maintained."

Jesus said: "He who seeks to preserve his life will lose it; but whoever loses his life on account of me will preserve his life." **Epictetus** said: "Socrates cannot be preserved by an act that is shameful. . . . It is dying that preserves him, not fleeing."

Jesus said: "Salt is good, but if the salt loses its savor, how can it be salted again? It is good neither for the land nor for the manure heap, and they throw it out." **Epictetus** said: "Why have you made yourself so useless and worthless? . . . When some household article has been thrown out intact and serviceable, anyone who finds it will pick it up and prize it. But no one will do that."

There are other gospel sayings relevant to the Cynic hypothesis. The Mission Charge (Matt. 10:5–16; Mark 6:7–12; Luke 9:1–5; 10:1–12) sketches Christian itinerants as resembling Cynic wanderers to the point that the minor differences are usually taken to denote attempts to distinguish the two kinds of mendicant preachers since they were so easy to confuse. And if the only differences you could point out were so picky, think how similar these scarecrows must have been!

A few sayings credited to Jesus can be read as partaking in the irreverence of Cynics toward conventional religion. When Jesus defends his dubious habit of associating publicans and sinners with the retort: "It is the sick who need the doctor, isn't it? Not the healthy," it may sound a bit different when you read that, when spotted coming out of a whorehouse, Diogenes said, "When the sun's light penetrates an outhouse, is it thereby polluted?" Likewise, in the much-commented on Corban controversy of Mark 7, Jesus' punch-line seems to lampoon the fastidious scruples of the Pharisees: "But it all winds up in the toilet anyway!"

An anecdote involving Guru Nanak, the fifteenth-century founder of the Sikh religion, perfectly captures the Cynic spirit:

Leaving Delhi they proceeded on to the Ganges where, as it happened to be a festival day, they observed thousands of people bathing in the river. The festival which was being celebrated was that of Baisakhi, and the pilgrims were throwing water in the direction of the rising sun. Guru Nanak also entered the river and began splashing water in the opposite direction. This provoked offended demands for an explanation. The Guru responded by asking his questioners to whom they thought they were conveying water and they replied that they were sending it to their ancestors in heaven. Guru Nanak then informed them that he was, in the same manner, watering his fields in Lahore. When this brought a scornful rejoinder he answered that if their water could travel as far as heaven his could certainly reach Lahore.[228]

The Buddha, too, could be found in a Cynic mood. In explaining the early Buddhist suspicion of show-off miraculous stunts, Edward Conze[229] supplies the following anecdote.

> One day the Buddha came across an ascetic who sat by the bank of a river, and who had practiced austerities for 25 years. The Buddha asked him what he had got out of all his labour. The ascetic proudly replied that now at last he could cross the river by walking on the water. The Buddha tried to point out that this was little gain for so much labour, since for one penny the ferry would take him across.[230]

But the key thing is the admonitions ascribed to Jesus in which he demands that disciples sell off their possessions and donate the cash to the poor (Mark 10:21; Luke 14:33). You can come up with rabbinical sayings that parallel the Jesus and the Cynic sayings about divine provision for birds and animals, but who but the Cynics urged total divestiture? If Jesus used to say stuff like this, he was a Cynic. And, as Burton Mack says, "The Cynic analogy repositions the historical Jesus away from a specifically Jewish sectarian milieu and toward the Hellenistic ethos known to have prevailed in Galilee."[231]

---

228. W.H. McLeod, *Guru Nanak and the Sikh Religion* (Delhi: Oxford University Press, 1968), p. 55.

229. Edward Conze, *Buddhism: Its Essence and Development.* Harper Colophon Books (New York: Harper & Row, 1975), pp. 104–105. Thanks to my friend Vairochana Asura for tracking this down for me!

230. Of course I realize that my examples from Guru Nanak and the Buddha show that a sage need not have been a Cynic to be a cynic, so Jesus need not have been either.

231. Mack, p. 73.

8 THE LOGOS AS THE LOTUS

To suggest significant Buddhist influence upon Christianity is by no means new,[232] but more recently scholars led by the late Christian Lindtner[233] and Michael Lockwood[234] have contended that Christianity and Essene monasticism originated as "indigenized" versions of Buddhism by Buddhist missionaries sent to Egypt and Syria by Emperor Asoka in the third century B.C.E. Lindtner and Zacharias P. Thundy suggest that Philo's Egyptian ascetics, the *Thera*peutae, were Buddhist *Thera*vadins.

> *Therapeuta* is the Hellenization of the Sanskrit/Pali word *theravada*; they were probably the successors of the missionaries whom Emperor Asoka sent to Egypt, to the kingdom of Ptolemy, in the

232. Albert J. Edmunds, *Buddhist & Christian Gospels: Being Gospel Parallels from Pali Texts* (Yuhokwan Publishing House, 1908); Arthur Lillie, *The Influence of Buddhism on Primitive Christianity* (London: Swan Sonnenschein & Co., 1893); Dwight Goddard, *Was Jesus Influenced by Buddhism? A Comparative Study of the Lives and Thoughts of Gautama and Jesus* (Thetford, VT, 1927).

233. Christian Lindtner, *Geheimnisse um Jesus Christus: Das Neue Testament ist Buddhas Testament*. Internationale Literatur zur Erforschung politischer Hintergrundmächte, Band 10 (Süderbrarup: Lühe-Verlag, 2005).

234. Michael Lockwood, ed., *Buddhism's Relation to Christianity: A Miscellaneous Anthology with Occasional Comment* (Tambaram, Channai: Tambaram Research Center, 2010).

third century as Theravada medical missionaries.[235]

Likewise, according to Lindtner, *Simon Peter* was the same as the Buddha's favorite disciple *Sariputtra*. When "Jesus moved from Nazaret to Kapernaoum, [it has been] derived from *Kapilavastu-nagarât* (the ablative form)."[236] Jesus "went to be baptized by John the Baptist, for that was the way 'to fulfill all righteousness' - the ten Greek syllables translate the ten Sanskrit syllables: *sarvajnatâdharmaparipirîm*, also accusative, found in the Prajnâ-pâramitâ."[237] And so forth.

Did Christianity, or, if one prefers, the Christian gospel (in either sense: message or story), somehow grow out of the *Saddharma-Pundarika* (the Lotus of the True Law) and other Buddhist scriptures? The question is reminiscent of the Buddhist belief that, when one with esoteric knowledge beholds the Buddha, he sees the towering form of the Superman. The form available to the gaze of all others is the Nirmankya, or Transformation body, while that seen only by the enlightened is the Sambogkya, the Glorified body of the Buddha as he exists on the Celestial plane. Even so, many, hearing of the hypothesis of Buddhist influence on Christian origins, see but a highly contrived theory, while others, willing to examine the question in a deeper and wider manner, have found in the *Lotus Sutra* a revelation concerning gospel/Christian origins. The question is seen to be as great and imposing as the divine form of the Tathagata, and I aim to narrow the focus to one particular facet here.

The visit of the shepherds, alerted by angels to the advent of the baby savior, is recounted in both traditions. The sky-filling angels of Luke provide a close parallel to the Buddhist story of the sage Asita,

---

235. Zacharias P. Thundy, *Buddha and Christ: Nativity Stories and Indian Traditions*. Studies in the History of Religions (*Numen* Bookseries. Vol. LX (Leiden: E.J. Brill, 1993), p. 245.

236. Christian Lindtner, correspondence with the present author, September 9, 2020.

237. Lindtner, correspondence with present author, July 6, 2019.

which in turn would appear to have suggested Luke's story of the oracle of Simeon (Luke 2:25–35). Prince Siddhartha has just been born, and his ostensible father King Suddhodana sought the aid of diviners to predict the destiny of the child.

> And at that time on the side of a peak of the Himalayas dwelt a great sage named Asita. . . . At the moment when the Bodhisattva was born he beheld many marvelous wonders: the gods over the space of the sky making the word 'Buddha' resound, waving their garments, and coursing hither and thither in delight. . . . So the great sage Asita . . . rose up and flew through the air to the great city of Kapilavatthu, and on arriving, laid aside his magic power, entered Kapilavatthu on foot, arrived at the abode of King Sud-dhodana, and stood at the door of the house. . . . Then the king taking the boy . . . in both hands brought him into the presence of the sage. Thus Asita observing beheld the Bodhisattva endowed with the thirty-two marks of a great man and adorned with the eighty minor marks, his body surpassing that of Sakra, Brahma, and the world-protectors with glory surpassing a hundred and thousand-fold, and he breathed forth this solemn utterance: 'marvellous verily is this person that has appeared in the world,' and rising from his seat clasped his hands, fell at the Bodhisattva's feet, made a rightwise circuit round, and taking the Bodhisattva stood in contemplation. [He then predicts the two possible careers of the child, as a world conqueror or a world-redeemer.] And looking at him he wept, and shedding tears, sighed deeply. The king beheld Asita weeping, shedding tears, and sighing deeply. And beholding him the hair of his body rose, and in distress he hastily said to Asi-ta, 'why, O sage, dost thou weep and shed tears, and sigh deeply? Surely there is no misfortune for the boy?' At this Asita said to the king, 'O king, I weep not for the sake of the boy . . . , but I weep for myself. And why? I, O king, am old, aged, advanced in years, and this boy . . . will no doubt attain supreme complete enlightenment. And having done so will turn the supreme Wheel of Doctrine that

has not been turned by ascetic or brahmin, or god, or Mara, or by any other in the world; for the weal and happiness of the world he will teach the Doctrine. . . . But we shall not see that Buddha-jewel. Hence, O king, I weep, and in sadness I sigh deeply, for I shall not be able to reverence him."

Like Simeon, Asita embodies all the faithful of past centuries, having lived long enough to glimpse, but *just* to glimpse, the Desire of Ages finally come. Whereas Simeon rejoices to have gotten even this peek, Asita is sorrowful he will see no *more* than a peek, but the metaphor is the same. And it is not too much to suggest that the Christian story has been borrowed from the Buddhist.[238] Derrett denies the Buddhist origin of the Simeon parallel, but Zacharias P. Thundy[239] rejects this, noting that the Buddhist nativity parallels are easily early enough to be primary.

It has long been apparent that the Q (Matthean/Lukan) Temptation narrative parallels similar legends about Abraham, Zoroaster, and the Buddha. Any of these stories might have been derived from any of the others, or they may be independent spontaneous creations of what Martin Dibelius called the "law of biographical analogy."[240] But there is an interesting clue in Luke's version suggesting a Buddhist origin. Here, but not in Matthew's version, the devil asserts his sovereignty over all the kingdoms of the world (Luke 4:6b). This matches the Buddhist characterization of Mara the Tempter, who rules the material world with its riches and delights. Mara knows that, if the Buddha succeeds, he stands to lose a lot of business! And this has carried over into the Lukan version.

238. Edward J. Thomas, *The Life of Buddha as Legend and History* (London: Routledge & Kegan Paul, 1927), pp. 39–41; Thundy, *Buddha and Christ*, pp. 115–116.

239. Thundy, *Buddha and Christ*, p. 76.

240. Martin Dibelius, *From Tradition to Gospel*. Trans. Bertram Lee Woolf. Scribner Library (New York: Scribners, n.d.), pp. 108–109.

Mark's version of the Temptation (Mark 1:1:12–13) lacks any propositions by Satan. Nor does it even imply Jesus is fasting. Rather, he is being served (food) by angels, recalling Elijah's wilderness retreat (1 Kings 17:6; 19:5–8). It also recalls a moment in Prince Siddhartha's ruminations concerning the futility of austerities.

> I thought: "Suppose I were to practice going altogether without food?" Then angels (*devas*) came to me and said, "Dear sir, please don't practice going altogether without food. If you go altogether without food, we'll infuse divine nourishment in through your pores, and you will survive on that." I thought, "If I were to claim to be completely fasting while these angels are infusing divine nourishment in through my pores, I would be lying." So I dismissed them, saying, "Enough."[241]

Probably the most spectacular pre-Easter miracle attributed to Jesus is his walking on the jade pavement of the Lake of Galilee. This, too, has what looks like a Buddhist prototype.

> The incident occurred during the rainy season when water was falling so violently from the skies that it was soon no longer possible to walk around dry-footed. Gautama was not interested in going for a walk but rather in meditating while walking. Special paths were established in monasteries for this important Buddhist practice. Gautama used his extraordinary abilities to keep [this] area free of water so that he could meditate. Kassapa was much concerned about the revered teacher. Fearful that the Awakened One could be swept away by the raging waters, he jumped into a boat to seek him. Then he saw . . . Gautama . . . walking on the water [to meet him] without getting wet. Kassapa was so surprised that he first disbelievingly asked: "Are you there, great mendicant monk?" With the words "It is I, Kassapa" the Buddha calmed the

---

241. Majjhima-Nikaya 36 (Mahasaccakasutta). Trans. Thanissaro Bhikku. In Lockwood, p. 39.

fearful man and came to the boat.[242]

We even have the detail of the disciple in the boat asking for confirmation of the apparition's identity, as well as the same reply. But it doesn't stop there. Matthew's gospel adds to Mark's version a sequel in which Peter gets his turn to stroll atop the waves. He seems to reason that, if Jesus is not a ghost, even though he appears to be weightless, he ought to be able to cause Peter, too, to walk on water. So he exits the boat and does walk on the waves—until he realizes what he is doing and starts to sink like the rock he is named for. Jesus steadies him and rebukes him for his lack of faith. The lesson, of course, is that a Christian must not waver in his faith in a time of trouble but focus on his Lord and all will be well. This lesson is expressed even more clearly in this Buddhist tale, possibly the original.

> He arrived at the bank of the river Aciravati in the evening. As the ferryman had drawn the boat up on the beach, and gone to listen to the Doctrine, the disciple saw no boat at the ferry, so finding joy in making Buddha the object of his meditation he walked across the river. His feet did not sink in the water. He went as though on the surface of the earth, but when he reached the middle he saw waves. Then his joy in meditating on the Buddha grew small, and his feet began to sink. But making firm his joy in meditating on the Buddha, he went on the surface of the water, entered the Jetavana, saluted the Teacher, and sat on one side (Introduction to Jataka Tale 190).[243]

As if we did not have enough versions of Jesus' adoration by a grateful weeping woman, Buddhist scriptures provides still another.

---

242. Madhavagga, summarized by Elmar R. Gruber and Holger Kersten, *The Original Jesus: The Buddhist Sources of Christianity* (Rockford: Element Books, 1996), pp. 98–99.

243. Thomas, *Life of Buddha as Legend and History*, p. 241.

Kasyapa said [to Ananda]: "Thou didst show to corrupt women the golden body of the Blessed One, which was then sullied by their tears." "I thought," replied Ananda, "that if they then but saw the Blessed One, many of them would conceive a longing to become like him." Kasyapa said again, "Because you did not prevent the woman polluting the feet of Buddha, you were guilty of a dukkata (offence), and you should now confess and repent of it." Ananda replied, "A woman with a tender heart worshipping at Buddha's feet, her tears falling fast upon her hands, soiled the (sacred) feet as she held them to her. In this I am conscious of no crime; nevertheless, venerable sir! In submission to your judgment, I now confess and repent."[244]

This one is especially striking. It parallels the stories of Jesus' anointing, even to the feature of a disciple complaining about a woman's maudlin gesture of devotion, which is associated with the Master's death, shortly before in Jesus' case, shortly after in the Buddha's. This seems an improbable combination of narrative elements to find in a Christian *and* a Buddhist story. It goes well beyond the law of biographical analogy.

Bultmann[245] admitted that the following Buddhist version of the Samaritan Woman story was very likely borrowed from Buddhism, but Lindtner and Lockwood go all the way to saying the Johannine version bears the same relation to the Buddhist version that Matthew does to Mark—both within the same scriptural stream.

---

244. W. Woodville Rockhill, trans., *The Life of the Buddha and the Early History of his Order: Derived from Tibetan Works in the Bkah-Hgyur and Bstan-Hgyur: Followed by Notices on the Early History of Tibet and Khoten* (London: Kegan Paul, Trench, Trübner & Co. Ltd., 1907), p. 154; Samuel Beal, *Four Lectures on Buddhist Literature in China* (London, 1882), p. 75. Quoted in Lockwood, p. 45.

245. Rudolf Bultmann, *The Gospel of John: A Commentary.* Trans, G.R. Beasley-Murray, R.W.N. Hoare, and J.K. Riches (Philadelphia: Westminster Press, 1971), p. 179, n. 4.

The Master was sojourning near Sravasti, and Ananda used to enter the town daily on his begging round. Once as he was returning from the town, he became thirsty and saw a Chandala maiden, named Prakrati, fetching water from a well. "Sister," he said to her, "give me some water to drink." Prakriti replied, "I am a Chandala girl [an Untouchable caste], revered Ananda." "Sister," said Ananda, "I do not ask you about your family and your caste, but if you have any water left, give it to me and I will drink." [246] (An *avadana* story translated from Sanskrit into Chinese in 265 C.E.)

From this point the Buddhist story goes in a different direction from the Johannine version, but not completely. In the former, Prakriti falls hopelessly in love with Ananda and wishes to marry him. The marriage theme is represented in John 4 by the business of the Samaritan's husband(s).

The other great gospel story of a Samaritan, that of the Good Samaritan who rescued a Jew mugged and left for dead in the ditch, possesses a striking Buddhist parallel, too.

Here it is said that a young Brahmin was staying in a hostel for young brahmins ... but he fell ill with vomiting and diarrhea. Rather than attend to him, however, the others, "from fear of pollution" ... threw him out and abandoned him. It is only the Buddhist monks Sariputra and Maudgalyayana who, when they chanced upon him, "cleaned him with a bamboo brush, rubbed him with white earth and bathed him." Because they also "taught" the Dharma for him—and here this almost certainly can refer only to a kind of deathbed recitation—he died in a good state of mind and was reborn in heaven.[247]

---

246. Lockwood, p. 74.

247. Gregory Schopen, *Buddhist Monks and Business Matters: Still More Papers on Monastic Buddhism in India* (Honolulu: University of Hawaii Press, 2004), pp. 7–8. Quoted in Lockwood, p. 78.

There, obviously, is the familiar interreligious element: the abandoned Hindu is rescued by Buddhists, like Luke's battered Jew saved by a heretical Samaritan. But there is also the matter of the pious clerics' indifference to a man's suffering because they are preoccupied with the niceties of ritual purity, implied, as many think, in Luke but explicit here. The Buddhist version can almost count as confirmation of that particular reading of Luke—as if we are reading the original version. Maybe we are. Here's another.

> Pokkharasati said to Ambattha, "Gautama is staying in the deep jungle. And concerning that Blessed Lord a good report has been spread about: 'This Blessed Lord is a fully enlightened Buddha.' Now you go see the ascetic Gautama and find out whether this report is correct or not, and whether the Reverend Gautama is as they say or not." Digha Nikya 3:1:4)[248]

Of course we have to think of the imprisoned John the Baptist hearing about Jesus and summoning his disciples to go check him out. Really, it's the same story and, again, nothing we would necessarily expect from the law of biographical analogy.

If, as Lindtner and Lockwood hold, Jesus was the literary reincarnation of Gautama Buddha, he seems to have inherited a particular outreach strategy. If Jesus made inroads among the community of sinners and rogues (Matt. 9:10–13), so had the Buddha.

> The Bodhisattva made his appearance at the fields of sports and in the casinos, but his aim was always to mature those people who were attached to games and gambling. . . . To demonstrate the evils of desire, he even entered the brothels. To establish drunkards in correct mindfulness, he entered all the taverns. (Vimalakirti-nirdesa Sutra 2)[249]

---

248. In Lockwood, p. 82.
249. In Lockwood, p. 82.

In John 7:38 Jesus is shown claiming he is fulfilling some unnamed verse of scripture: "Whoever believes on me, as the scripture has said, out of his belly shall flow rivers of living water." *Scrip*ture? *What* scripture? There is certainly nothing in the Old Testament that the evangelist could have been referring to. Albert Joseph Edmunds[250] decided that the scripture must be this one. "In this case, the Tathagato works a twin miracle unrivalled by disciples: from his upper body proceeds a flame of fire, and from his lower body proceeds a torrent of water (Patisambhida-maggo I. 53). J. Duncan M. Derrett[251] deemed a Buddhist origin improbable, partly because the Johannine version makes no mention of fire, but this may have been omitted by the evangelist given that he was adapting it to the context of the Feast of Tabernacles, associated with the pouring of water

GOTAMA AND GOLGOTHA

In older treatments of the Christ Myth theory, one sometimes runs across the claim that the Buddha was (said to have been) crucified.[252] There is no evidence that any Buddhists ever believed this, but there *is* interesting evidence seemingly relevant to the case. A major Buddhist source for the Passion Narrative might be the *Mula-Sarvastivada-Vinaya*,[253] which recounts the impalement of the innocent Gautama (an ancestor of Gautama Buddha) for the murder of a prostitute named Bhadra, whose actual killer had slipped away in

---

250. Albert Joseph Edmunds, *Buddhist Texts Quoted as Scripture by the Gospel of John: A Discovery in the Lower Criticism.* Classic Reprint Series (1906; rpt. Forgotten Books, 2012), p. 9.

251. J. Duncan M. Derrett, *The Bible and the Buddhists.* Nonum Supplementum Bibbia e Oriente (Casa Editrice Sardini, 2000), pp. 41–42.

252. E.g., Kersey Graves, *The World's Sixteen Crucified Saviors* (1875; rpt. New Hyde Park: University Books, 1971), pp. 115–116.

253. Zacharias P. Thundy, *The Trial of Jesus and his Death on the Cross: Buddhist Sources of Gospel Narratives* (2015), chapter four, "Passion and Death of Gautama and of Jesus," pp. 120–161.

the crowd. As Gautama is dying slowly in agony, his old teacher approaches, and the two have a last talk. Gautama is dismayed that he will leave no sons behind. It begins to rain, and the water (identified with semen) mixes with Gautama's dripping blood as it falls to the ground. The story presupposes ancient Indian embryology, pre-scientific by our standards, so that we read that a pair of eggs developed from the mixed drops, and the shells broke, eventually growing into two posthumous sons for Gautama. His old mentor adopts them.

> Gautama Rishi said, "Teacher, when I have departed this life, what will become of me? What will my future rebirth be?" [His teacher] answered, "Son, Brahmins say that without sons, one sinks into non-existence. Have you offspring?" [Gautama:] "Teacher, I am only a young man, without knowledge of the ways of women. Although my father wanted me to inherit the kingdom, I became a mendicant. How would I have offspring?" [Teacher:] "Son, if that is so, you should try to recall the experience of sexual pleasure [from a previous life]." [Gautama:] "Teacher, right now terrible pains overwhelm me, my vital organs are pierced, my joints loosened, and my mind is focused on approaching death. How can I recall the experience of sexual pleasure [in a previous life]?" His teacher had acquired the Five Superhuman Faculties. By means of these he created a great downpour. The raindrops fell on [Gautama's] body. Thanks to a cool, wet wind, his pains were alleviated. He began to recall an experience of sexual pleasure [in a previous life]. Due to this recollection of sexual pleasure, two drops of semen mixed with blood fell [on the ground]. . . . The two drops of semen metamorphosed into two eggs. When the sun rose and heated them they cracked open. Two princes were born.[254]

We have, then, a "crucified" martyr. The impalement stake takes the place of both Jesus' cross and the centurion's stabbing spear in John 19:34. The mixing of Gautama's blood with the rain water cor-

---

254. In Lockwood, pp. 271, 273.

responds to the water and the blood draining from the ribs of Jesus in John 19:34. Gautama is dying in the place of an actual criminal, a killer, just as Jesus dies in place of the killer Barabbas. The word used for the "shells" (*kapalani*)[255] of the embryonic eggs is also used for "skulls," which brings to mind Golgotha, "the place of skulls." But the capper is that the Sanskrit phrase for "two-water-drops-with-blood" is *dvau sukra-bindu sa-rudhire*. So? Sanskrit and Greek are, of course, cognate languages. The word *sa-rudhire* becomes the Greek *kai Rouphou*, "and red." "Rufus" means "red." The name "Alexander" (actually taking a genitive ending here, hence *Alexandrou*) is trans-literated from the Sanskrit *sukra-bindu*. Thus *dvau sukra-bindu sa-rudhire* transliterates to *Alexandrou kai Rouphou*. Odd as it sounds, this would solve the puzzle of Mark 15:21: who are "Alexander and Rufus," and why are they mentioned? In Mark, they are the sons of Simon of Cyrene; in the Gautama version, they are the sons of the impaled man.[256] What are the chances that all this is mere coincidence, outrageous as it must strike us, captive as we are to conventional assumptions?

One of the most astonishingly strange passages in scripture is Matthew 27:51–53. "And behold, the curtain of the temple was torn in two, from top to bottom; and the earth shook, and the rocks were split; the tombs also were opened, and many bodies of the saints who had fallen asleep were raised, and coming out of the tombs after his resurrection they went into the holy city and appeared to many."[257] Perhaps it is a variant of a Buddhist story.

---

255. Also, think of the cosmic container shells of Kabbalistic cosmogony, called *Kelipoth*.

256. The Gnostic Basilides would have said it makes perfect sense, since he took Mark to be saying Simon had been crucified in Jesus' place! If this were so, then both crucified/impaled men had sons named Alexander and Rufus!

257. I cannot help mentioning an interesting explanation of this text offered by Jehovah's Witnesses who, as I understand it, say these verses mean simply that the Matthean earthquake which split rocks and broke open mau-

A Buddha is sitting inside a stupa and he calls out: Good, Good Sakyamuni![258] . . . All those who are present are amazed. Where does the voice come from? Who is the man inside the stupa? With his finger, Sakyamuni then tears the cover in two, not from top to bottom, but from bottom to top. Inside the stupa, we now see, is an emaciated Buddha. He was the one who cried out in Sanskrit: *Sadhu, sadhu, Sakyamuni!* Now we begin to understand why "Jesus", "from the cross", cried: *Eli, Eli. La ' ma sabach-tha'-ni!* The Buddhist source then goes on to relate how the earth shakes, how the rocks split and how the tombs were opened and an enormous number of so-called bodhisattvas, holy men, emerged from the earth. Coming up from the earth . . . they went up to the stupa, where the two Buddhas were now sitting together. . . . They promise to help spread the "Gospel of the Lotus Sutra"—the source of all these events.[259]

Derrett says: "The coincidence of earthquake and saints coming out of caves, etc., is too much. Can this conjunction have been invented more than once?"[260]

A GATHERING OF VULTURES

The Lotus Sutra is, of course, a Sermon on the Mount, but given the

---

soleums also bounced recently interred corpses out onto the open ground (as often happens with flooding). Relatives of the departed arrived to check for damage and were naturally dismayed to behold the decaying remains of their loved ones exposed to public view. Of course that is not quite what the verses say, but it would make a lot of sense if this version was the original and that some redactor decided to up the supernatural ante by making the dead emerge alive like Lazarus and knock on the doors of home, as in "The Monkey's Paw" by W.W. Jacobs.

258. This is an epithet of the Buddha meaning "the Sage of the Sakya clan," to which he belonged.

259. Lockwood, pp. 280–281.

260. Derrett, p. 74.

basic structures of sacred space, it is no surprise to find revelation issuing from the Axis Mundi,[261] whether Gautama or Jesus is the conduit. The scene need hardly have been borrowed by Matthew from this Buddhist text (though it might have been). What I find notable here is the hint of kinship between the Buddha's Vulture Peak and a Q text from Luke and Matthew. The version in Luke 17:33–37 is especially interesting:

> "Whoever may try to save his life, he will lose it, and whoever will let it go, he will preserve it. I tell you, in this night, there will be two on one couch; the one will be taken and the other will be left! There will be two grinding grain together; the one will be taken, but the other will be left! There will be two in the field; the one will be taken, and the other will be left!" And answering, they say to him, "Taken where, Lord?" And he said to them, "Where do you think? You'll find the body where the vultures are circling."

The vultures gather, as they do in the *Saddharma-Pundarika*, the birds of prey symbolizing the numerous saints, seers, and bodhisattvas (who, with a grain of Kierkegaardian cynicism, might be viewed as carrion birds waiting to feast on the spiritual remains of their master, soon to depart from this life!) assembled to attend the Buddha's instruction. What he is about to do is to set spinning the wheel of the Mahayana Dharma. And here I must think of the gospel image of grinding the grain, i.e., *turning the mill wheel.* Has someone misunderstood the Buddhist metaphor of turning the wheel of the Dharma and made it into an example of common work to be interrupted by the apocalyptic crisis? It is not frivolous to ask this question in view of the fact that Luke 17:33 warns of the inevitability of forfeiting one's (presumably) precious *psuche* ("soul," "life," "self") by the very act of seeking to secure it. Is that not the danger from which the *anatta*, no-atman, no-self, no-soul doctrine is designed to rescue us?

---

261. Eliade, *Sacred and the Profane*, pp. 36–39.

THE PARALLEL SON

To many Christians, the Lukan parable of the Prodigal Son is practically the canon-within-the canon, defining their view of the essence both of the Christian religion broadly and of their Christian duty. Would it matter to Christians if the parable was Buddhist in origin?[262] That would not make it uniquely Buddhist, somehow not Christian, in character.[263] In any event, a good case can be made that the Buddhist parable of a lost son in *Lotus Sutra* chapter IV forms the prototype for Luke's version. Luke's counts as the longest of his parables. There are important differences, true, but the correspondences are astonishing, all the more so if we insist there is no genetic connection.

> It is a case, O Lord, as if a certain man went away from his father and betook himself to some other place. He lives there in foreign parts for many years, twenty or thirty or forty or fifty. In course of time the one (the father) becomes a great man; the other (the son) is poor; in seeking a livelihood for the sake of food and clothing he roams in all directions and goes to some place, whereas his father removes to another country. The latter has much wealth, gold,

---

262. Lillie, *Influence of Buddhism on Primitive Christianity*, pp. 70–71, credits the original to Buddhism, as does Rudolf Seydel (*Das Evangelium von Jesu in seinen Verhältnissen zu Buddha-sage und Buddhe-lehre* (Leipzig, 1882), p. 230. Incredibly, Charles Francis Aiken, in his *The Dhamma of Gotama the Buddha and the Gospel of Jesus the Christ* (Boston: Marlier, 1900), pp. 225–226, denies that the two stories even deserve to be called parallels. Derrett, *Bible and the Buddhists*, p. 65, thinks the Lukan parable was first, and that Buddhists borrowed it. Just the opposite of my reading, Derrett regards the Buddhist moral of the story as artificial and "far from clear," thus secondary. Derrett there reviews other opinions as well, including that the two parables are spontaneous and independent, or that, while neither copies from the other, both share some common ultimate source.

263. It would not be a case analogous to the work of the Pseudo-Dionysius the Areopagite, the acceptance of which under its canonical pseudonym smuggled an alien Neo-Platonism into Christianity.

corn, treasures, and granaries; possesses much (wrought) gold and silver, many gems, pearls, lapis lazuli, conch shells, and stones(?), corals, gold and silver; many slaves male and female, servants for menial work. and journeymen; is rich in elephants, horses, carriages, cows, and sheep. He keeps a large retinue; has his money invested in great territories, and does great things in business, money-lending, agriculture, and commerce.

In course of time, Lord, that poor man, in quest of food and clothing, roaming through villages, towns, boroughs, provinces, kingdoms, and royal capitals, reaches the place where his father, the owner of much wealth and gold, treasures and granaries, is residing. Now the poor man's father, Lord, the owner of much wealth and gold, treasures and granaries, who was residing in that town, had always and ever been thinking of the son he had lost fifty years ago, but he gave no utterance to his thoughts before others, and was only pining in himself and thinking: "I am old, aged, advanced in years, and possess abundance of bullion, gold, money and corn, treasures and granaries, but have no son. It is to be feared lest death shall overtake me and all this perish unused." Repeatedly he was thinking of that son: "O how happy should I be, were my son to enjoy this mass of wealth!"

Meanwhile, Lord, the poor man in search of food and clothing was gradually approaching the house of the rich man, the owner of abundant bullion, gold, money and corn, treasures and granaries. And the father of the poor man happened to sit at the door of his house, surrounded and waited upon by a great crowd of Brâhmans, Kshatriyas, Vaisyas, and Sûdras; he was sitting on a magnificent throne with a footstool decorated with gold and silver, while dealing with hundred thousands of kotis of gold-pieces, and fanned with a chowrie, on a spot under an extended awning inlaid with pearls and flowers and adorned with hanging garlands of jewels; sitting (in short) in great pomp. The poor man, Lord, saw his own father in such pomp sitting at the door of the house, surrounded with a great crowd of people and doing a householder's business. The poor man frightened, terrified, alarmed, seized with a feeling of horripilation all over the body, and agitated in mind, reflects thus: "Unexpectedly have I here fallen in with a king or grandee. People like me have nothing to do here; let me go; in the street of the poor I am likely to find food and clothing without much difficulty. Let me no longer tarry at this place, lest I be taken to do forced labour or incur some other injury."

Thereupon, Lord, the poor man quickly departs, runs off, does not tarry from fear of a series of supposed dangers. But the rich man, sitting on the throne at the door of his mansion, has recognised his son at first sight, in consequence whereof he is content, in high spirits, charmed, delighted, filled with joy and cheerfulness. He thinks: "Wonderful! He who is to enjoy this plenty of bullion, gold, money and corn, treasures and granaries, has been found! He of whom I have been thinking again and again, is here now that I am old, aged, advanced in years."

At the same time, moment, and instant, Lord, he dispatches couriers, to whom he says: "Go, sirs, and quickly fetch me that man." The fellows thereon all run forth in full speed and overtake the poor man, who, frightened, terrified, alarmed, seized with a feeling of horripilation all over his body, agitated in mind, utters a lamentable cry of distress, screams, and exclaims: "I have given you no offence." But the fellows drag the poor man, however lamenting, violently with them. He, frightened, terrified, alarmed, seized with a feeling of horripilation all over his body, and agitated in mind, thinks by himself: "I fear lest I shall be punished with capital punishment; I am lost." He faints away, and falls on the earth. His father dismayed and near despondency says to those fellows: "Do not carry the man in that manner." With these words he sprinkles him with cold water without addressing him any further. For that householder knows the poor man's humble disposition and his own elevated position; yet he feels that the man is his son.

The householder, Lord, skilfully conceals from every one that it is his son. He calls one of his servants and says to him: "Go, sirrah, and tell that poor man: 'Go, sirrah, whither thou likest; thou art free."' The servant obeys, approaches the poor man and tells him: "Go, sirrah, whither thou likest; thou art free." The poor man is astonished and amazed at hearing these words; he leaves that spot and wanders to the street of the poor in search of food and clothing. In order to attract him the householder practises an able device. He employs for it two men ill-favoured and of little splendour. "Go," says he, "go to the man you saw in this place; hire him in your own name for a double daily fee, and order him to do work here in my house. And if he asks: 'What work shall I have to do?' tell him: 'Help us in clearing the heap of dirt.'" The two fellows go and seek the poor man and engage him for such work as mentioned. Thereupon the two fellows conjointly with the poor man clear the heap of dirt in the house for the daily pay they receive from the rich man, while they take up their abode in a hovel of straw in the neighbourhood of the rich man's dwelling. And that rich man beholds through a window his own son clearing the heap of dirt, at which sight he is anew struck with wonder and astonishment.

Then the householder descends from his mansion, lays off his wreath and ornaments, parts with his soft, clean, and gorgeous attire, puts on dirty raiment, takes a basket in his right hand, smears his body with dust, and goes to his son, whom he greets from afar, and thus addresses: "Please, take the baskets and without delay remove the dust." By this device he manages to speak to his son, to have a talk with him and say: "Do, sirrah, remain here in my service; do not go again to another place; I will give thee extra pay, and whatever thou wantest thou mayst confidently ask me, be it the price of a pot, a smaller pot, a boiler or wood, or be it the price of salt, food, or clothing. I have got an old cloak, man; if thou shouldst want it, ask me for it, I will give it. Any utensil of such sort, when thou wantest to have it, I will give thee. Be at ease, fellow; look upon me as if I were thy father, for I am older and thou art younger, and thou hast rendered me much service by clearing this heap of dirt, and as long as thou hast been in my service thou hast never shown nor art showing wickedness, crookedness, arro-

gance, or hypocrisy; I have discovered in thee no vice at all of such
as are commonly seen in other man-servants. From henceforward
thou art to me like my own son."

From that time, Lord, the householder addresses the poor
man by the name of son, and the latter feels in presence of the
householder as a son to his father. In this manner, Lord, the householder affected with longing for his son employs him for the clearing of the heap of dirt during twenty years, at the end of which
the poor man feels quite at ease in the mansion to go in and out,
though he continues taking his abode in the hovel of straw.

After a while, Lord, the householder falls sick, and feels that
the time of his death is near at hand. He says to the poor man:
"Come hither, man, I possess abundant bullion, gold, money and
corn, treasures and granaries. I am very sick, and wish to have one
upon whom to bestow (my wealth); by whom it is to be received,
and with whom it is to be deposited. Accept it. For in the same
manner as I am the owner of it, so art thou, but thou shalt not suffer anything of it to be wasted."

And so, Lord, the poor man accepts the abundant bullion,
gold, money and corn, treasures and granaries of the rich man,
but for himself he is quite indifferent to it, and requires nothing
from it, not even so much as the price of a prastha of flour; he
continues living in the same hovel of straw and considers himself
as poor as before.

After a while, Lord, the householder perceives that his son
is able to save, mature and mentally developed; that in the consciousness of his nobility he feels abashed, ashamed, disgusted,
when thinking of his former poverty. The time of his death approaching, he sends for the poor man, presents him to a gathering
of his relations, and before the king or king's peer and in the presence of citizens and country-people makes the following speech:
"Hear, gentlemen! this is my own son, by me begotten. It is now
fifty years that he disappeared from such and such a town. He is
called so and so, and myself am called so and so. In searching after
him I have from that town come hither. He is my son, I am his

father. To him I leave all my revenues, and all my personal (or private) wealth shall he acknowledge (his own)."

The poor man, Lord, hearing this speech was astonished and amazed; he thought by himself: "Unexpectedly have I obtained this bullion, gold, money and corn, treasures and granaries."

Even so, O Lord, do we represent the sons of the Tathâgata, and the Tathâgata says to us: "Ye are my sons," as the householder did. We were oppressed, O Lord, with three difficulties, viz. the difficulty of pain, the difficulty of conceptions, the difficulty of transition (or evolution); and in the worldly whirl we were disposed to what is low. Then have we been prompted by the Lord to ponder on the numerous inferior laws (or conditions, things) that are similar to a heap of dirt. Once directed to them we have been practising, making efforts, and seeking for nothing but Nirvâna as our fee. We were content, O Lord, with the Nirvâna obtained, and thought to have gained much at the hands of the Tathâgata because of our having applied ourselves to these laws, practised, and made efforts. But the Lord takes no notice of us, does not mix with us, nor tell us that this treasure of the Tathâgata's knowledge shall belong to us, though the Lord skilfully appoints us as heirs to this treasure of the knowledge of the Tathâgata. And we, O Lord, are not (impatiently) longing to enjoy it, because we deem it a great gain already to receive from the Lord Nirvâna as our fee. We preach to the Bodhisattvas Mahâsattvas a sublime sermon about the knowledge of the Tathâgata; we explain, show, demonstrate the knowledge of the Tathâgata, O Lord, without longing. For the Tathâgata by his skilfulness knows our disposition, whereas we ourselves do not know, nor apprehend. It is for this very reason that the Lord just now tells us that we are to him as sons, and that he reminds us of being heirs to the Tathâgata. For the case stands thus: we are as sons to the Tathâgata, but low (or humble) of disposition; the Lord perceives the strength of our disposition and applies to us the denomination of Bodhisattvas; we are, however, charged with a double office in so far as in presence of Bodhisattvas we are called persons of low disposition and at the same time have to rouse them to Buddha-enlightenment. Knowing the strength of our disposition the Lord has thus spoken, and in this way, O Lord, do we say that we have obtained unexpectedly and without longing the jewel of omniscience, which we did not desire, nor seek, nor search after, nor expect, nor require; and that inasmuch as we are the sons of the Tathâgata.

Luke's version reads like a truncation of the more complex Buddhist original (supposing for a moment that the *Lotus Sutra* version is original). Whereas, in the Buddhist parable, the awakening of the son is a long and difficult process, so deeply has the son sunk into Samsaric befuddlement, Luke has the son suddenly snap out of it. The difference corresponds with that between the "Catholic" character of Luke, who simply calls sinners to repent, and the Gnostic character of the *Saddharma-Pundarika*, which here implicitly prescribes a difficult discipline leading to awakening to the forgotten secret of one's own sonship (Buddha-nature). Indeed, the point of the Buddhist parable might be summed up well in saying 3b of the Gospel according to Thomas: "If you will only know yourselves, then you will be known, and you will know that you are the sons of the Living Father. But if you do not know yourselves, then you are mired in poverty, and you are that poverty." Luke elsewhere displays an anti-Gnostic agenda,[264] and it may be he has truncated the parable with this in mind. Note the somewhat clumsy result: the returned son is not clearly repentant at all. We need see no more in his soliloquy than a clever stratagem. His father could never forgive him, but even if he hired him as a laborer, he would be better off; it's worth a try! Judge for yourself.

And he said, "A certain man had two sons. And the younger of the two said to the father, 'Father, give me the share of the property

---

264. Charles H. Talbert, *Luke and the Gnostics: An Examination of the Lucan Purpose* (New York: Abingdon Press, 1966).

that falls to me.' And he divided the living between them. And after not many days, the younger son, having packed his things, left for a distant country, and there squandered his property with a life of excess. When he had spent everything, a severe famine hit that country, and he began to feel the pinch. And he went looking for work and attached himself to one of the citizens of that country, and he sent him into his fields to feed the pigs. And he longed to ease his hunger with the husks that the pigs ate, and no one gave him food. And one day he came to his senses, and he said, 'How many of my father's hirelings have plenty of loaves, but as for me, here I am, dying of hunger! I will get up and go to my father, and I will say to him, 'Father, I sinned against heaven and before you. No longer am I worthy to be called a son of yours. Demote me to be one of your hirelings.' And getting up, he began the journey to his father. But while he was still far away, his father saw him and was touched with pity and ran to his son, embracing him and kissing him tearfully. And the son said to him, 'Father, I sinned against heaven and before you; no longer am I worthy to be called a son of yours . . .' But the father said to his slaves, 'Quickly! Bring out the best robe and clothe him, and put a ring on his hand and sandals on his feet, and bring the fattened calf, kill it, and let us celebrate with a feast! Because this son of mine was dead and lived again, was lost and found!' And they began to celebrate. But his older son was in a field; and as he came near the house, he heard music and dancing. And calling over one of the serving boys, he asked what was going on. And he said to him, 'Your brother has arrived, and your father killed the fattened calf, because he got him back safe and sound!' But he was furious and refused to enter, so his father came out and pleaded with him. But answering, he said to the father, 'Behold, as many years as I served you, never in all that time disobeying a single order from you, and to me you never allowed me a goat so that I might feast with my friends! But when this son of yours arrived, after consuming your living with prostitutes, you killed the fattened calf in his honor!' And he said to him, 'My child, you are always with me, and whatever I have is

yours. But it was only proper for us to rejoice because your brother was dead and came to life, and having been lost, was also found!'"
(Luke 15:11–32)

BEFORE BRAHM-A WAS, I AM

As David Friedrich Strauss observed,[265] the apparently self-aggrandizing speeches of Jesus in the Fourth Gospel, which, when taken literally as the speech of a historical individual, lead to inevitable questionings of his sanity,[266] is really a brilliantly effective type of devotional idiom, according to which the paeans heaped on the object of worship by the worshipper are fictively placed on the lips of the one worshipped, so to create an invitation, model, and magnet for the adulation of which the object is thus declared worthy. The overflowing piety and imagination of the devotee causes him or her to declare, "You are the light of the world!" "You are the only way to the Father!" But the gospel writer, seeking to awaken such adoration, depicts the glorified Christ as declaiming in his own right: "I am the light of the world!" "I am the way, the truth, and the life—no one comes to the Father but by *me*!" The same technique occurs elsewhere, e.g., in the Isis Aretalogy, in which the god-queen is depicted as singing her own divine praises.[267] The *Bhagavad Gita* furnishes further examples. We find such thrilling I-revelations in the *Lotus Sutra*, too. For instance, in chapter V.

---

265. David Friedrich Strauss, *The Life of Jesus for the People* (London: Williams & Norgate, 1879), Vol. I, pp. 209, 272–273.

266. Albert Schweitzer points out the danger of attributing such sayings to the historical Jesus in his dissertation *The Psychiatric Study of Jesus: Exposition and Criticism.* Trans. Charles R. Joy (Boston: Beacon Press, 1948), p.41.

267. Philip B. Harner, *The "I Am" of the Fourth Gospel.* Facet Books Biblical Series 26 (Philadelphia: Fortress Press, 1970), pp. 26–27. Harner rejects the Isis parallel proposed by Deissmann, but only by splitting hairs, in my opinion.

I am the Tathâgata, O ye gods and men! the Arhat, the perfectly enlightened one; having reached the shore myself, I carry others to the shore; being free, I make free; being comforted, I comfort; being perfectly at rest, I lead others to rest. By my perfect wisdom I know both this world and the next, such as they really are. I am all-knowing, all-seeing. Come to me, ye gods and men! Hear the law. I am he who indicates the path; who shows the path, as knowing the path, being acquainted with the path.

Compare this with John 14:66: "Jesus says to him, 'I am the way! And the truth and the life! No one comes to the Father except by me!'" And with Matthew 11:28–30: "And to the crowd he said, 'Come to me, all those laboring under heavy burdens, and I will relieve you! Take my yoke on your shoulders instead, and learn my doctrine, for I am meek and humble in heart, no taskmaster, and you shall find rest for your souls; for my yoke is easy to bear, and the burden I assign is light.'"

We can almost see the process in motion before us when we compare two texts, one Buddhist, the other Christian. *Saddharma-Pundarika* VII: 54 addresses its devotional predicates to the Buddha: "Hail! thou art come at last, O Light of the world! thou, born to be bounteous towards all beings." But John 8:12 puts them in the mouth of Jesus himself: "I am the light of the world! Whoever follows me will never grope about in darkness, but will have the light of life!"

Is there sufficient reason to make the Jesus-revelations dependent upon the Buddhist versions? We already have our answer: the instincts of piety appear to be universal, and it would have clothed itself in such colors independently wherever it might arise. On the other hand, the more striking correspondences one finds between Buddhist and Christian texts and terminology, the more seriously one must consider the possibility of direct inheritance. It is a cumulative case, involving numerous interlocking bits of data.

THE BLIND MEN AND THE ELEPHANT
IN THE MIDDLE OF THE ROOM

Chapter V of *The Lotus Sutra* anticipates John chapter 9 in startlingly specific ways.

> I will tell thee a parable, for men of good understanding will gen-
> erally readily enough catch the meaning of what is taught under
> the shape of a parable. It is a case, Kâsyapa, similar to that of a cer-
> tain blind-born man, who says: "There are no handsome or ugly
> shapes; there are no men able to see handsome or ugly shapes;
> there exists no sun nor moon; there are no asterisms nor plan-
> ets; there are no men able to see planets." But other persons say
> to the blind-born: "There are handsome and ugly shapes; there
> are men able to see handsome and ugly shapes; there is a sun and
> moon; there are asterisms and planets; there are men able to see
> planets." But the blind-born does not believe them, nor accept
> what they say. Now there is a physician who knows all diseases.
> He sees that blind-born man and makes to himself this reflection:
> The disease of this man originates in his sinful actions in former
> times. All diseases possible to arise are fourfold: rheumatical, cho-
> lerical, phlegmatical, and caused by a complication of the (cor-
> rupted) humours. The physician, after thinking again and again
> on a means to cure the disease, makes to himself this reflection:
> "Surely, with the drugs in common use it is impossible to cure
> this disease, but there are in the Himalaya, the king of mountains,
> four herbs, to wit: first, one called Possessed-of-all-sorts-of-co-
> lours-and-flavours; second, Delivering-from-all-diseases; third,
> Delivering-from-all-poisons; fourth, Procuring-happiness-to-
> those-standing-in-the-right-place. As the physician feels compas-
> sion for the blind-born man he contrives some device to get to the
> Himalaya, the king of mountains. There he goes up and down and
> across to search. In doing so he finds the four herbs. One he gives
> after chewing it with the teeth; another after pounding; another

after having it mixed with another drug and boiled; another after having it mixed with a raw drug; another after piercing with a lancet somewhere a vein; another after singeing it in fire; another after combining it with various other substances so as to enter in a compound potion, food, &c. Owing to these means being applied the blind-born recovers his eyesight, and in consequence of that recovery he sees outwardly and inwardly, far and near, the shine of sun and moon, the asterisms, planets, and all phenomena. Then he says: "O how foolish was I that I did not believe what they told me, nor accepted what they affirmed. Now I see all; I am delivered from my blindness and have recovered my eyesight; there is none in the world who could surpass me." And at the same moment Seers of the five transcendent faculties [the five senses], strong in the divine sight and hearing, in the knowledge of others' minds, in the memory of former abodes, in magical science and intuition, speak to the man thus: "Good man, thou hast just recovered thine eyesight, nothing more, and dost not know yet anything. Whence comes this conceitedness to thee? Thou hast no wisdom, nor art thou a clever man." Further they say to him: "Good man, when sitting in the interior of thy room, thou canst not see nor distinguish forms outside, nor discern which beings are animated with kind feelings and which with hostile feelings; thou canst not distinguish nor hear at the distance of five yoganas the voice of a man or the sound of a drum, conch trumpet, and the like; thou canst not even walk as far as a kos without lifting up thy feet; thou hast been produced and developed in thy mother's womb without remembering the fact; how then wouldst thou be clever, and how canst thou say: 'I see all'? Good man, thou takest darkness for light, and takest light for darkness."

Whereupon the Seers are asked by the man: "By what means and by what good work shall I acquire such wisdom and with your favour acquire those good qualities (or virtues)?" And the Seers say to that man: "If that be thy wish, go and live in the wilderness or take thine abode in mountain caves, to meditate on the law and cast off evil passions. So shalt thou become endowed with the virtues of an ascetic and acquire the transcendent faculties." The man catches their meaning and becomes an ascetic. Living in the wilderness, the mind intent upon one sole object, he shakes off worldly desires, and acquires the five transcendent faculties. After that acquisition he reflects thus: "Formerly I did not do the right thing; hence no good accrued to me. Now, however, I can go whither my mind prompts me; formerly I was ignorant, of little understanding, in fact, a blind man."

Such, Kâsyapa, is the parable I have invented to make thee understand my meaning. The moral to be drawn from it is as follows. The word "blind-born," Kâsyapa, is a designation for the creatures staying in the whirl of the world with its six states; the creatures who do not know the true law and are heaping up the thick darkness of evil passions. Those are blind from ignorance, and in consequence of it they build up conceptions; in consequence of the latter name-and-form, and so forth, up to the genesis of this whole huge mass of evils.

So the creatures blind from ignorance remain in the whirl of life, but the Tathâgata, who is out of the triple world, feels compassion, prompted by which, like a father for his dear and only son, he appears in the triple world and sees with his eye of wisdom that the creatures are revolving in the circle of the mundane whirl, and are toiling without finding the right means to escape from the rotation. And on seeing this he comes to the conclusion: Yon beings, according to the good works they have done in former states, have feeble aversions and strong attachments; (or) feeble attachments and strong aversions; some have little wisdom, others are clever; some have soundly developed views, others have unsound views. To all of them the Tathâgata skilfully shows three vehicles.

The Seers in the parable, those possessing the five transcendent faculties and clear-sight, are the Bodhisattvas who produce enlightened thought, and by the acquirement of acquiescence in the eternal law awake us to supreme, perfect enlightenment.

The great physician in the parable is the Tathâgata. To the blind-born may be likened creatures blind with infatuation. Attachment, aversion, and infatuation are likened to rheum, bile, and phlegm. The sixty-two false theories also must be looked upon as such (i.e. as doshas, "humours and corrupted humours of the body," "faults and corruptions"). The four herbs are like vanity (or voidness), causelessness (or purposelessness), unfixedness, and reaching Nirvâna. Just as by using different drugs different diseases are healed, so by developing the idea of vanity (or voidness), purposelessness, unfixedness, (which are) the principles of emancipation, is ignorance suppressed; the suppression of ignorance is succeeded by the suppression of conceptions (or fancies); and so forth, up to the suppression of the whole huge mass of evils. And thus one's mind will dwell no more on good nor on evil.

To the man who recovers his eyesight is likened the votary of the vehicle of the disciples and of Pratyekabuddhas. He rends the ties of evil passion in the whirl of the world; freed from those ties he is released from the triple world with its six states of existence. Therefore the votary of the vehicle of the disciples may think and speak thus: "There are no more laws to be penetrated; I have reached Nirvâna." Then the Tathâgata preaches to him: "How can he who has not penetrated all laws have reached Nirvâna?" The Lord rouses him to enlightenment, and the disciple, when the consciousness of enlightenment has been awakened in him, no longer stays in the mundane whirl, but at the same time has not yet reached Nirvâna. As he has arrived at true insight, he looks upon this triple world in every direction as void, resembling the produce of magic, similar to a dream, a mirage, an echo. He sees that all laws (and phenomena) are unborn and undestroyed, not bound and not loose, not dark and not bright. He who views the profound laws in such a light, sees, as if he were not seeing, the whole triple world full of beings of contrary and omnifarious fancies and dispositions.

John 9:1–41:

And, passing by, he noticed a man blind from birth. And his disciples asked him, saying, "Rabbi, who sinned, this poor wretch or his parents, that he was born blind?" Jesus answered, "Neither this man nor his parents sinned; he was born blind so that the mighty works of God might be displayed through him.. We are obliged to engage the tasks set by the one who sent me while there is still daylight left, for night is closing in, when no one can work. While I linger in the world, I am the light of the world." Having said these things, he spat on the ground and made mud with the saliva, and he smeared the mud on his eyes, and said to him, "Go, wash it off in the Pool of Siloam," which is translated as "the one sent." So he went and washed and came back seeing. Therefore his neighbors and those who used to see him begging said, "Surely this isn't the one who used to sit and beg?" Some said, "It's him, all right!" Others said, "No, it can't be! He just looks like him!" The man confirmed, "It is I!" So they said to him, "Then how were your eyes opened?" He answered, "The man named Jesus made mud and anointed my eyes with it and told me, 'Go to Siloam and wash.' So I went, and when I washed, I could see!" And they said, "Where is that man?" He says, "I do not know." They led him to the Pharisees, the once-blind man. Now the day Jesus made the mud and opened his eyes was a sabbath.

So once again the Pharisees asked him how he saw again. And he said to them, "He smeared mud on my eyes, and I washed it off, and now I see." So some of the Pharisees said, "This man is not from God, because he does not observe the sabbath!" But others said, "How can a sinful man perform such signs?" And there was a division among them. Therefore they turned to the blind man again, saying, "Well, what do you have to say about him? It was your eyes that he opened!" And he said, "He is a prophet!" Therefore the Jewish authorities did not believe that he was blind and then saw, until they sent for the parents of the man who could now see and asked them, "Is this your son, whom you say was born blind? If so, how does he see now?" So his parents answered and said, "We know that this is our son, and that he was born blind, but how it is that he now sees, we do not know, or, for that matter, who opened his eyes we do not know. Ask him! He is of age and can speak for himself!" His parents said these things because they feared the rulers of the Jews, for the rulers of the Jews had already agreed that if anyone would confess him as Christ, they would be ejected from the synagogue. That is why his parents said, "He is of age; ask him."

So a second time they summoned the man who was blind and enjoined him, "Give glory to God, now! We know that this man is a sinner." So that one answered, "He may be a sinner for all I know. But one thing I know: having been blind, I now see!" So they said to him, "What exactly did he do to you? How did he open your eyes?" He answered them, "I told you already, but I guess you didn't hear me! Why do you want to hear it again? Do you want to become his disciples as well?" And they reviled him and said, "You are a disciple of that fellow! We are disciples of Moses! We know that God has spoken by Moses, but as for this fellow? We do not even know who he represents." The man answered and said to them, "Here's the miracle! You don't know whether he comes from God, despite the fact that he opened my eyes! We know that God does not hear the prayers of sinners, but if anyone is pious toward God and obeys his will, he will be heard. From ages past, no one ever heard of anyone opening the eyes of the congenitally blind. So if this fellow were not from God, he could never do such a thing." They retorted and said to him, "You son of a whore! You think you can lecture us?" And they threw him into the street.

Jesus heard that they threw him out, and, finding him, they said, "Do you believe in this man?" That one answered and said, "Point him out to me, Lord, that I may know which one to believe in!" Jesus said to him, "You're looking at him right now, and he is the one talking with you!" And he said, "Lord, I do believe!" And he bowed before him. And Jesus said, "I came into this world to render judgment, so that those who do not see may see and the sighted may go blind." Some of the Pharisees who were with him heard this and said to him, "Oh, so we're blind, too?" Jesus said to them, "If you were blind, you wouldn't be responsible; but now that you say, 'We can see just fine,' your guilt remains."

We are at once struck with the occurrence in both stories, not only of the fairly obvious and irresistible metaphor of physical blindness standing for spiritual blindness, but even more with the question of karmic antecedents to congenital blindness of the former sort. A man is born blind for his own sins left over from a previous life. To find this theme in the Johannine version is already practically a sufficient argument for a Buddhist original, given the alienness of the karma-and-samsara theme in gospel-era Judaism.[268] Neither Jesus nor his questioning disciples seem to think the possibility of being *born* blind as a punishment for *past* sins is anything untoward (though no one in John's text commits himself to this verdict). This requires a scenario in which karma and reincarnation are simply taken for granted.

There is a group of ostensibly holy men in both stories, the Pharisees in the one, the Seers in the other. The savior is present in both stories, though he is but the narrator in *The Lotus Sutra* and does not come on stage, while in John, he is an important character among the dramatis personae. But the relationship between the holy men and the recovered blind man is altogether different. The Seers seek to aid in the blind man's enlightenment, whereas in John they try to pretend it did not happen, in order to discredit the healer. Yet even this function is intended to highlight the effect of the miracle and the extent of the healing, since the Pharisees' opposition only galvanizes the once-blind man in his determination to confess the Son of Man.

In both versions we find a scale of relative blindness. The Pharisees possess physical vision but are lost in spiritual darkness for their

---

268. Lillie, *Influence of Buddhism on Primitive Christianity*, p. 55, accents the parallel, insisting that Jesus here refers to reincarnation. But he takes the passage as literal history and thus as evidence that contemporary Jews already believed in reincarnation.

opposition to Jesus. In *The Lotus Sutra* parable, the blind man himself represents still another holy group, the bodhisattvas who had not awakened to the full truth but now have. They may be compared to the Pharisees in John, for whom Jesus seems to hold out no hope. Why? In their religious arrogance, they have chosen not to advance beyond their spiritual mediocrity since that would imply their present level of attainment is less than they would like to believe, and they cannot entertain the possibility that they are not virtuosos. In the end, however, the polemical point is pretty much the same: John leaves the spiritually blind in their chosen fog of half-truths, while the Buddhist parable aims its edge at those who stand by what the parable calls the second-rate truths of the arhats and the Pratyeka-buddhas. I should say the similarity of the two stories is at least as great as that between John chapter 4's story of the Samaritan Woman at the well and the Buddhist episode of Ananda and the Candala caste woman, which seems manifestly to be a Christian borrowing from a Buddhist source.[269]

And, speaking of John chapter 4, we find another fascinating parallel, this time regarding the superiority of spiritual nourishment over physical for the enlightened. Concerning them, the *Saddharma-Pundarika*, chapter VIII:19 relates: "They shall know no other food but pleasure in the law and delight in knowledge." Likewise, in John 4:31–34, we read how "the disciples urged him, saying, 'Rabbi, eat! Eat!' But he said to them, 'I have food to eat that you are un-

---

269. The Agamas. The story is available in Jack Kornfield, ed., *Teachings of the Buddha* (rev. ed., New York: Barnes & Noble Books, 1996), pp. 105–106. Rudolf Bultmann drew attention to the use of a Buddhist source here in *The Gospel of John: A Commentary*, p. 179, but he despairs of deciding one way or the other whether the Christian version is based on the Buddhist, despite the affirmations of various previous students of the question, such as G.A. van den Bergh van Eysinga, *Indische Einflüsse auf evangelische Erzählungen*, 1932, pp. 60–62. Lillie, p.p. 72–73, sees it, too. As to a possible Buddhist origin for John chapter 9, though, Bultmann rejects it (*History of the Synoptic Tradition*, p. 427): "Fantastic!" Really? Derrett thinks the two versions have influenced one another in various stages, whichever had the germ first (*Bible and the Buddhists*, pp. 68–69).

aware of.' Therefore the disciples said to one another, 'Surely no one brought him food while we were gone?' Jesus says to them, 'My food is doing the will of the one who sent me, and finishing his work.'" In both cases we may wonder whether, in this sovereign indifference to physical food, we glimpse a sign of the glorified, "docetic" Superman whose semblance to the fleshly condition is merely a visual aid.

ARE WE THERE YET?

I cannot help recognizing (or, some may say, imagining) a striking parallel between *Lotus Sutra* VIII:33 and Thomas 18.

> On hearing from the Lord the announcement of their own future destiny, the five hundred Arhats, contented, satisfied, in high spirits and ecstasy, filled with cheerfulness, joy, and delight, went up to the place where the Lord was sitting, reverentially saluted with their heads his feet, and spoke thus: We confess our fault, O Lord, in having continually and constantly persuaded ourselves that we had arrived at final Nirvâna, as (persons who are) dull, inept, ignorant of the rules, for, O Lord, whereas we should have thoroughly penetrated the knowledge of the Tathâgatas, we were content with such a trifling degree of knowledge.
>
> The disciples say to Jesus, "Tell us our destiny!" Jesus says, "Oh, does that mean you have discovered your origin, that you ask about your destiny? For where your origin is, there, too, shall be your destiny. Blessed is the one who shall arrive at the beginning, for he shall know the end, and he shall not taste death."

The two passages share a premature eagerness on the part of enthusiastic disciples who want to know in advance their destiny, the degree of their eschatological glorification, perhaps their degree of reward in the hereafter, or how long it is going to take for complete spiritual attainment. In this desire the disciples only show their immaturity. The more anxiety one feels for the question, the further behind one is in his or her progress toward that end. They did not yet know as they should have known and, in effect, sought to leap-frog the required process of growth which itself constitutes the only way of knowing the answer they seek. I think the comparison is no mere parallel; it seems to me that the disciples' question makes sense only in the context which *The Lotus Sutra* provides. In Thomas, the Christian reader is left wondering not only why the disciples want to know their destiny (as opposed to John 21:21–22, where a jealous disciple wants to know instead about the future in store for a rival disciple, not his own), but also what sort of answer they might have expected from Jesus in the first place.

By the way, what is the point of enumerating the labors and degrees of glory in store for the various Buddhist heroes and saints in *The Lotus Sutra*? I have to assume it is a way of ranking the various bodhisattvas, akin to stipulating which apostle founded which church, catechizing each church's bishop, in short, a pedigree of ecclesiastical clout. The rank assigned the various Buddhas and bodhisattvas must have been reflected in the prestige accorded various monasteries or even latter-day saints who claimed to embody the *tulkus* of these ancient companions of the Buddha.

OMNISCIENT BUT FORGETFUL

Lotus Sutra VIII:36 tells a tale quite similar to that in chapter IV, in which a man has forgotten his identity amid the stupor of worldly squalor.

> It is, O Lord, as if some man having come to a friend's house got drunk or fell asleep, and that friend bound a priceless gem within his garment, with the thought: "Let this gem be his." After a while, O Lord, that man rises from his seat and travels further; he goes to some other country, where he is befallen by incessant difficul-

ties, and has great trouble to find food and clothing. By dint of great exertion he is hardly able to obtain a bit of food, with which (however) he is contented and satisfied. The old friend of that man, O Lord, who bound within the man's garment that priceless gem, happens to see him again and says: "How is it, good friend, that thou hast such difficulty in seeking food and clothing, while I, in order that thou shouldst live in ease, good friend, have bound within thy garment a priceless gem, quite sufficient to fulfil all thy wishes? I have given thee that gem, my good friend, the very gem I have bound within thy garment. Still thou art deliberating: 'What has been bound? by whom? for what reason and purpose?' It is something foolish, my good friend, to be contented, when thou hast with (so much) difficulty to procure food and clothing. Go, my good friend, betake thyself, with this gem, to some great city, exchange the gem for money, and with that money do all that can be done with money." In the same manner, O Lord, has the Tathâ-gata formerly, when he still followed the course of duty of a Bo-dhisattva, raised in us also ideas of omniscience, but we, O Lord, did not perceive, nor know it.

The story might have served for the inspiration of the *Hymn of the Pearl*, a bit of Gnostic liturgy embedded in the Syriac *Acts of Thomas*.[270] I supplied the text in my section on the Gnostic Redeem-er, above. The major difference between the two works is that, in the *Lotus Sutra* version, the recipient of the (spiritual) wealth does not know he has been given the gift, while in the Gnostic *Hymn*, the re-cipient first knew of the treasure entrusted him, but then forgot and had to be awakened to his endowment and his mission. But is there really much of a difference? Probably not: both are but different ways of stressing the fact that the average person, even the seeker, actually possesses knowledge that he does not know he has. How did it get there? That is what one has to discover. And there is still another text,

---

270. Translated by G.R.S. Mead.

Thomas, saying 109, which underlines the point more concisely:

> Jesus says, "The kingdom is like a man who had a treasure buried in his field without knowing it. When he died, he left it to his son. The son did not know about it either, and once he inherited the field, he sold it. And he who bought it went to it and, while plowing, discovered the treasure. He began lending money to whomever he wished."

Thomas' version implies the ignorant passage from one unfulfilled life to another, via reincarnation, till one "cashes in."

CUTTING THE MUSTARD

Though both Mark 4:31–32 and *Saddharma-Pundarika* XI:48 contain a parable of the mustard seed, they first appear to be making entirely different points.

> In the whole universe there is not a single spot so small as a mustard-seed where [the future Buddha] has not surrendered his body for the sake of creatures. Afterwards he arrived at enlightenment. Who then would believe that she should have been able to arrive at supreme, perfect knowledge in one moment?
>
> As a grain of mustard which, when one sows it on the ground, is smaller than all the seeds on the earth but, once it germinates, comes up and becomes greater than all the herbs and makes great branches so that the birds of the sky are able to find lodging in its shadow.

But on second thought, perhaps they are not so different after all. Both appear to teach that a great salvation may be the result of a long, long period of spiritual endeavor beginning from miniscule antecedents. Has Mark's version grown from *The Lotus Sutra*? If so, it would seem to be the product of a long process of oral transmission rather than direct borrowing and rewriting.

TRANSCENDENCE AND TRANSEXUALISM

Whether modern readers are able to hear them with the ears of the ancients, we cannot say, but certain texts clash almost unbearably with our modern sensibilities, especially what appear to be grossly androcentric texts like the following.

> Then the venerable Sariputra said to that daughter of Sagara, the Naga-king: "Thou hast conceived the idea of enlightenment, young lady of good family, without sliding back, and art gifted with immense wisdom, but supreme, perfect enlightenment is not easily won. It may happen, sister, that a woman displays an unflagging energy, performs good works for many thousands of Æons, and fulfils the six perfect virtues (Pâramitas), but as yet there is no example of her having reached Buddhaship, and that because a woman cannot occupy the five ranks, viz. 1. the rank of Brahma; 2. the rank of Indra; 3. the rank of a chief guardian of the four quarters; 4. the rank of Kakravartin; 5. the rank of a Bodhisattva incapable of sliding back."
>
> Now the daughter of Sâgara, the Nâga-king, had at the time a gem which in value outweighed the whole universe. That gem the daughter of Sâgara, the Naga-king, presented to the Lord, and the Lord graciously accepted it. Then the daughter of Sâgara, the Nâga-king, said to the Bodhisattva Pragñâkûta and the senior priest Sariputra: "Has the Lord readily accepted the gem I presented him or has he not?" The senior priest answered: "As soon as it was presented by thee, so soon it was accepted by the Lord." The daughter of Sâgara, the Nâga-king, replied: "If I were endowed with magic power, brother Sariputra, I should sooner have arrived at supreme, perfect enlightenment, and there would have been none to receive this gem."

At the same instant, before the sight of the whole world and of the senior priest Sariputra, the female sex of the daughter of Sâgara, the Naga-king, disappeared; the male sex appeared and she manifested herself as a Bodhisattva, who immediately went to the South to sit down at the foot of a tree made of seven precious substances, in the world Vimala (i.e., spotless), where he showed himself enlightened and preaching the law, while filling all directions of space with the radiance of the thirty-two characteristic signs and all secondary marks. (*Lotus Sutra* XI: 51)

Simon Peter says, "Tell Mariam to leave us, because women are unworthy of the Life." Jesus says, "Behold, I shall lead her to make her male, so that she, too, may become a living spirit, like you males. For every woman who makes herself male will enter the kingdom of heaven." (Thomas 114)

What strikes us first, I dare say, is the phallocentric fanaticism that would disqualify women from spiritual qualification, and then the bizarre manner in which the text seeks to transcend the very cultural bias it displays. I can only say that the two texts' jolting two-steps-forward, one-step-backward attempts to vindicate the equality of women by, er, *making women into men* are so shocking, so weird, as to suggest one has been borrowed from the other. But perhaps it is merely my own modern bias that makes it look improbable for such sentiments to have been expressed independently.

DWELLERS UPON THE SUMMIT

I have always thought that if there is a Buddhist-influenced text in the gospels, this is it.

And after six days Jesus takes along Peter and James and John and leads them up into a high mountain solely by themselves. And he was metamorphosed in front of them, and his garments became blinding white, not merely the earthly whiteness of newly laundered clothes. And Elijah and Moses appeared to them, and they were engaged in conversation with Jesus. And Peter, reacting, says to Jesus, "Rabbi, it is good for us to be here! And let us make three shrines: one for you, one for Moses, and one for Elijah!" Actually, he did not know what response to make, for they became frightened out of their wits. And a cloud appeared, overshadowing them, and a voice was heard to speak from the cloud: "This one is my son, the beloved. Hear him!" And suddenly, as they looked around to see who it was who spoke, they no longer saw anyone with them except for Jesus alone. (Mark 9:2–8)

But is there any precedent for it in the *Saddharma-Pundarika*? Lillie[271] thought so, pointing to chapter XIV in which the Buddha reveals, despite expectation that he should long since have receded into richly deserved Nirvana, the great bodhisattva Lord Prabhutaratna: he continues on this side of the river to assist those who have not yet forded it. This passage has always put me in mind of the Christian Transfiguration.

---

271. Lillie, p. 63, points especially to Peter's reflex to erect commemorative stupas for the three saints.

PART THREE
COVENANT AND COMPROMISE

9 THE MAGIC APOSTLE

I have been attempting to demonstrate that, if we find unconvincing the now-standard picture of Jesus as something close to a Jewish rabbi, we are by no means left without a plausible alternative. Rather, we face an embarrassment of riches! There are so many tempting haystacks before me, the donkey, that I hardly know which to choose! Jesus might have been a Jewish makeover of Gautama Buddha. He might have been a man to whom the mythic trappings of the old Israelite/Judean Sacred King were applied, or an imaginative concretization of those old traditions. He could have been a historicized theophany or a figure, fictive or historical, in the shape of Enoch and other ancient deified biblical patriarchs. Then again, he might have been a historicized Gnostic Redeemer who had originally been pictured as undergoing a saving sacrificial death at the hands of primordial Archons. Any of these ought to be considered fair game, educated guesses about the identity of "Jesus." So, in a sense, I find myself convinced of *all* of them! And thus none of them, since I can't really render a verdict.

But I do have a proposal that would account for how and why a mythic Jesus would have come to be historicized, as well as explaining how, as a historian, one may understand the role of Paul and the Pauline gospel on the one hand and the Messianic Torah sect of James and Peter on the other, for they seem impossible to fit under

177

one roof. Remember how different the Pauline gospel was from the Synoptic version: what interest could the "good news" of the rightful king of a negligible postage stamp country have had for pagan Gentiles? Paul is said to have transformed the "Galilean gospel" into a Hellenistic mystery cult. But isn't it more natural to see here a fusion of two disparate sects?

> To the pagan converts ... what could a descendant of David mean? To them, Jesus became the actual Son of God, miraculously begotten, and sacrificed for the redemption of the world. (H.G. Enelow)[272]
>
> [The] shift [of the Christian movement outside Palestine occasioned] the winnowing out of aspects of Jewish Messianic thought. Such matters as the destruction of the Roman colonial power over Palestine and the restoration of a Jewish dynasty, with Jews reassembled from all over the world, scarcely had the same significance for Gentiles in Athens or in Rome as it had for Jews in Galilee." (Samuel Sandmel)[273]
>
> The Last Supper cannot be Jewish in origin. "[T]he sacramental words of the Last Supper, where the transubstantiation of wine and bread is proclaimed. It is apparent that this involved a later kerygma, in which Hellenistic mystery-cult elements, alien to Judaism, were integrated." (Schalom Ben-Chorin)[274]
>
> In any case, the imagery of eating a man's body and especially drinking his blood (Mark 14:22–24; Matt. 26:26–28; Luke 22:17–20), even after allowance has been made for metaphorical language, strikes a totally foreign note in a Palestinian Jewish cultural setting (cf. John 6:52). (Geza Vermes)[275]

---

272. H.G. Enelow, *A Jewish View of Jesus* (New York: Bloch Publishing Co., 1931), p. 162.

273. Sandmel, *We Jews and Jesus*, p. 35.

274. Schalom Ben-Chorin, *Brother Jesus*, p. 67.

275. Geza Vermes, *The Religion of Jesus the Jew* (Minneapolis: Fortress Press, 1993), p. 16.

Who was the Jerusalem Church? The sect of the Twelve, Jewish Christianity, was identical with the Qumran sect. Thus the council of twelve with an inner (or upper!) circle of three. To borrow a Shi'ite Islamic term, I propose calling this faction "the Twelvers."[276] And, as yet, there was no "Jesus" in the picture. Think of the common observation that, if the Twelve were supposed to be the tribal Patriarchs, where does Jesus fit in? He doesn't, because he is a subsequent insertion. From where? Suppose "Jesus" was originally the Marcionite/Paulinist Christ. The two sects merged, perhaps as part of a financial arrangement (as in Galatians). The narrative of Jesus as the Jewish Messiah was constructed by rewriting Old Testament stories. It was part and parcel of the "Catholicizing" phenomenon described by F.C. Baur. It started earlier, and more fundamentally, than he thought.

Ever since the discovery of the Dead Sea Scrolls in 1947, the remarkable parallels between the Qumran community and the Jerusalem Church have been glaringly evident; so much, in fact, that many scholars, as well as many non-specialists, dared to wonder if perhaps the two were one and the same. Was the mysterious "Teacher of Righteousness" really Jesus? In one sense such speculations were nothing new, since some of the parallels had already been apparent from the descriptions of the Essenes by Pliny the Elder, Philo of Alexandria, and Josephus, who was himself a member for a while. But the Dead Sea Scrolls revealed new features, such as the just-mentioned Teacher as well as the council of twelve elders and the top triumvirate. Methods of esoteric scripture current at Qumran have illuminated New Testament (especially Matthean) exegetical techniques.[277] The Dead Sea sectarians knew pretty well the historical sense of scrip-

---

276. As you no doubt already know, this term properly refers to the predominant Shi'ite sect who trace the line of Imams to the twelfth one, Muhammad al-Mahdi, whom they expect to return one day, along with Jesus, to establish a universal Shi'ite theocracy. Something to look forward to, no?

277. Krister Stendahl, *The School of Saint Matthew and Its Use of the Old Testament* (Philadelphia: Fortress Press, 1968).

tural texts, but they could not believe scripture's relevance was over. There might be hidden messages buried in the Bible if one could only learn how to discover them, to interpret those "sealed up" revelations. In exactly this way, Matthew surely knew that Hosea 11:1, "Out of Egypt have I called my son," was referring to Israel's exodus from Egypt, yet he cites it as a proof text for the Holy Family tip-toeing back into Judea once the post-Herod coast was clear. Was he cynically citing texts out of context in order to hoodwink pious readers who had no ready access to a copy of scripture to check for themselves? Before the 1947 discovery, some thought so.[278] But once we saw what the Qumran exegetes were doing, we realized Matthew was doing the same thing. It's not the same rules we play by, but back then that was the only game in town.

The communal lifestyle at Qumran immediately makes one think of the description of the Jerusalem Church in Acts 2:44–46 ("And all who believed were together and had all things in common; and they sold their possessions and distributed them to all, as any had need.") and 4:32 ("Now the company of those who believed were of one heart and soul, and no one said that any of the things which he possessed was his own, but they had everything in common."). Even Peter's voodoo killing of poor Ananias and Sapphira (Acts 5:1–11) for, despite their applause-getting announcement that they would liquidate their property for the common fund, secretly keeping back some of the money for a rainy day, recalls the severe punishments of rule-breakers at Qumran.

Similarly, Matthew stipulates procedures for intra-community transgressions or common quarrels: "If your brother sins against you, go and tell him his fault, between you and him alone. If he listens to you, you have gained your brother. But if he does not listen, take one or two brothers along with you, that every word may be

---

278. Joseph A. Wheless, *Is it God's Word? An Exposition of the Fables and Mythology of the Bible and of the Impostures of Theology* (New York: Alfred A. Knopf, 1926), chapter XIII, pp. 283–284.

confirmed by the evidence of two or three witnesses. If he refuses to listen to them, tell it to the church [*ecclesia*, i.e., summoned assembly]; and if he refuses to listen even to the church, let him be to you as a Gentile and a tax-collector" (Matt. 18:15–17). This is obviously the discipline of a cloistered brotherhood.

This is even clearer in the case of Matthew 5:22, "But I say to you that every one who is angry with his brother shall be liable to judgment; whoever insults his brother shall be liable to the council, and whoever says, 'You fool!' shall be liable to the hell of fire." In what society can someone be hauled into court for an unkind word? Obviously, we are here dealing with a tiny hot-house community so concerned with pious serenity that mere cross words constitute a serious crime. And the bar before which such cases are litigated is the board of rail-thin, bearded clerics in charge of such a conventicle. And is there any other scenario in which the verdict rendered to someone who had called a colleague "you empty-head!" would be consignment to *hell fire*? Presumably, these rules applied to the Qumran monastery, the in-town members (like today's Mennonites as opposed to their cousins the Amish, with whom they otherwise share many features), and the Jerusalem Church.

Perhaps the most astonishing of the Qumran scrolls is the apocalyptic War of the Sons of Light and the Sons of Darkness, essentially a battle plan for Armageddon, in which the brethren fully intended to participate. But until the appointed time, when the archangel's trumpet sounded, they were content to pray, get baptized every day, and study scripture. Though there was some overlap in doctrine and in membership between Essenes and Zealots, the chief difference was this, since the Zealots believed that God helps those who help themselves. Those who sit back and wait for God to save their sorry butts do not deserve his deliverance. It is precisely because of pious patience like that of the Essenes that the hour of deliverance is forever delayed! So the Zealots *acted*. I wonder if this is the original *Sitz-im-Leben* for Matthew 26:52–53. I suspect this saying originated as a revelation or fabrication from the Twelvers, arguing that the sect should not take the Zealot approach of violent revolt, but rather the approach mandated in the War Scroll, sitting back waiting for the arrival of warrior angels to ignite the Last Battle. Later on, once the Jesus figure was added to the picture, the saying was ascribed to the imagined heavenly Jesus speaking as if he could turn to the Father, enthroned to his left, and make the request, a la Wisdom 18:15 ("Thy all-powerful word leaped from heaven, from the royal throne, into the midst of the land that was doomed, a stern warrior."), for God to unleash his troops. Subsequently, once Jesus had been made into a "historical" figure, the saying would have been placed into the mouth of the human Jesus in Gethsemane. Note the number of the angelic reserves: *twelve* legions, one for each of the tribes and of the apostles. This sounds like the War Scroll to me.

Just to help the reader avoid becoming lost in terminology. Let me ask you to keep in mind that, throughout, I am referring to the Jerusalem Church, the Qumran community, the sect of John the Baptist, the Essenes, and the Ebionites as the same, or branches of the same, movement. As to identifying the Jerusalem Church/Ebionites with the Qumran community, I believe the pioneer of this theory was Jacob Teicher.[279] More recently it has been championed by Robert Eisenman.[280] These insights fit admirably well with the work of Etienne Nodet and Justin Taylor.

> Christianity emerged from among the Essenes, for whom baptism
> confirmed a process of initiation, and whose essential action as a
> community was an eschatological meal, principally of bread and

---

279. Jacob L. Teicher, *The Dead Sea Scrolls: Documents of the Jewish-Christian Sect of Ebionites* (1951). Teicher identified the Dead Sea Scrolls as the writings of the Jewish-Christian Ebionites, "the Poor," as in Galatians 2:10, where the reference is clearly to the Jerusalem Church.

280. Robert Eisenman, *James the Brother of Jesus: The Key to Unlocking the Secrets of Early Christianity and the Dead Sea Scrolls* (New York: Viking Press, 1997).

wine. Within this marginal culture a profound transformation came about, the decisive moment of which was contact with the Gentiles.[281] Renan, who of course could not know the discoveries that have accumulated since his time, was certainly correct to say that Christianity was an Essenism that has largely succeeded.[282]

Nodet and Taylor take an innovative and appropriately oblique approach, detecting puzzling inconsistencies between both baptism and the Eucharist on the one hand, and, on the other, the narrative or liturgical contexts in the New Testament in which they presently occur. For instance:

> Allusions to the Covenant and to blood (Matt 26:29 par.) strike a note which does not appear to be directly related to Passover, since there is no connection with the lamb, not even with the blood rite of Exod12:22 f. On the other hand, it has been noted for a long time now that the "Covenant blood" of Matt and Mark alludes to the sacrifice that seals the revelation at Sinai (Exod 24:8) [which therefore points instead towards Pentecost, celebrated at Qumran with bread and wine every fifty days.][283]

In the schema of Nodet and Taylor, these alterations in the sacraments of Essenism were the result of the introduction of the new Christian *kerygma* (the gospel preaching of cross and resurrection). The link with the "contact with the Gentiles," as we shall shortly see, means the encounter with *Paulinism*.

Suppose what would become "Jewish Christianity" originally had no Jesus/Messiah figure but rather was governed by a council of twelve, according cosmic significance to Peter (the foundation stone

---

281. Etienne Nodet and Justin Taylor, *The Origins of Christianity: An Exploration*. A Michael Glazier Book (Collegeville: Liturgical Press, 1998), back cover text.

282. Nodet and Taylor, p. 443.

283. Nodet and Taylor, pp. 112–113.

of the Temple/World)[284] and James and John (the Cosmic Pillars, sons of the Thunderer). The Twelve have been pushed aside exactly a la Noth's redundancy principle, whereby the addition of a new main character to a story, pushes the original protagonist(s) from center stage while not simply cutting them, instead reducing them to ancillary players.[285] Ditto for the three Pillars, made subordinate to Jesus. Their names attest/preserve their original cosmic (and non-Jesus) significance. John Allegro clarifies the meaning of the titles attached to James and John:

> GEShPU, "strong man", . . . forms the main part of the New Testament name for the brothers James and John, "Boanerges." The whole Sumerian phrase from which the Greek nickname comes was *GEShPU-An-Ur (read as *pu-an-ur-ges*) meaning "mighty man holding up the arch of heaven."[286]

This implies that James and John were myth-colored counterparts to the twins Castor and Pollux, sons of Zeus (the Thunderer), who were said to hold up the heavenly firmament. Further, the very notion of the three "pillars" as supreme authorities finds several echoes in Shi'ite Islam. And this, I believe, helps us to understand the original import of the Jerusalem triumvirate.

> Fatima, Ali, and their two sons, al-Hasan and al-Husayn [were the Prophet's relatives]. These four, with Muhammad, are exalted above the whole community of Islam, and no one in that community is equal to them in position or stature. They are regarded by the Shiites as the pillars of religion and the stronghold of the

---

284. Barker, *Gate of Heaven*, pp. 70–75.

285. Martin Noth, *A History of Pentateuchal Traditions*. Trans. Bernhard W. Anderson (Englewood Cliffs, N.J.: Prentice-Hall, 1972), pp. 162–166, 186.

286. John M. Allegro, *The Sacred Mushroom and the Cross: A Study of the Nature and Origins of Christianity within the Fertility Cults of the Ancient Near East* (New York: Bantam Books, 1971), pp. 100–101.

Islamic faith. Most significantly, only they, of all Muslims, are by rights heirs of the Prophet in leadership of the Islamic community.[287]

Shiites consider the Imams to be . . . the "pillars of Islam."[288]

The *qutb* (pole, axis) . . . [is] the highest spiritual authority. . . . He is considered the Star of Wisdom and the embodiment of the divine mysteries and teachings of the [Shabak] order. . . . He is not only the way that leads to the truth, he is the truth.[289]

These supporters of Ali are so important that the Shiites chose four men whom they called . . . Arkan (pillars), namely Salman, Abu Dharr, al-Miqdad Ibn al-Aswad, and Hdhayfa Ibn al-Yaman.[290]

In *Khutbat al-Bayan*, Ali claims to be . . . the upholder of heaven.[291]

WHO WAS PAUL?

As already anticipated, everything changed with the encounter of the Jerusalem/Qumran sect of the Twelvers with that of Paul. But this requires us to go back some steps to scrutinize Paul. I will summarize the arguments of F.C. Baur and Hermann Detering that "Paul" was none other than the infamous Simon Magus. Baur first recognized Paul as the alter ego of Simon in the fourth-century work, the Clementine Homilies, which contains a section of a second-century writing called the Preachings of Peter. In the following passage, we read

---

287. Matti Moosa, *Extremist Shiites: The Ghulat Sects* (Ithaca: Syracuse University Press, 1988), p. 81.

288. Moosa, p. 101.

289. Moosa, p. 89.

290. Moosa, p. 347.

291. Moosa, p. 180.

of a confrontation between Simon Peter and his arch-rival Simon Magus over the latter's claim to be no less an apostle than the former.

When Simon heard this, he interrupted [Peter] to say, "You assert that you thoroughly understand your teacher's concerns because, in his physical presence, you saw and heard him directly, but no one else could gain such understanding by means of a dream or a vision. But I shall show that this is false. One who hears something directly cannot be quite certain about what was said, for the mind must consider whether, being merely human, he has been deceived by the sense impression. But the vision, by the very act of appearing, presents its own proof to the seer that it is divine. First give me an answer to this."

And Peter said, "The prophet, once he has proved that he is a prophet, is infallibly believed in the matters which are directly spoken by him. Also, when his truthfulness has been previously recognized, he can give answers to the disciple, however the latter may wish to examine and interrogate him. But one who puts his trust in a vision or an apparition or dream is in a precarious position, for he does not know what it is he is trusting. For it is possible that it is an evil demon or a deceitful spirit, pretending in the speeches to be what he is not. Then if anyone should wish to inquire who it was who spoke, he could say of himself whatever he chose. Thus, like an evil flash of lightning, he stays as long as he chooses and then vanishes, not remaining with the inquirer long enough to answer his questions.

"Therefore it is not because God is jealous, but because he is merciful that he remains invisible to flesh-oriented man. For no one who sees can survive. For the extraordinary light would dissolve the flesh of the beholder, unless the flesh were changed by the ineffable power of God into the nature of light, so that it could see the light - or unless the light-substance were changed into flesh, so that it could be seen by flesh. For the Son alone is able to see the Father without being transformed. The case of the righteous is different: in the resurrection of the dead, when their bodies, changed into light, become like angels, then they will be able to see. Finally, even if an angel is sent to appear to a man, he is changed into flesh, that he can be seen by flesh. For no one can see the incorporeal power of the Son or even of an angel. But if someone sees a vision, let him understand this to be an evil demon. But it is obvious that impious people also see true visions and dreams, and I can prove it from scripture. . . . Thus the fact that one sees visions and dreams and apparitions by no means assures that he is a religious person. Further, to the pure and innate religious mind the truth gushes up, not eagerly courted by a dream, but granted to the good by intelligence. It was in this way that the Son was revealed to me by the Father. Therefore I know what the nature of revelation is, since I learned it myself. [Peter›s Caesarea Philippi confession in Matthew 16:13–16 is related, then Numbers 2;6–8.] . . . You see how revelations of anger are through visions and dreams, while those to a friend are mouth to mouth, by sight and not by puzzles and visions and dreams, as they are to an enemy. So even if our Jesus did appear in a dream to you, making himself known and conversing with you, he did so in anger, speaking to an opponent. That is why he spoke to you through visions and dreams - through revelations which are external. But can anyone be qualified by a vision to become a teacher? And if you say it is possible, then why did the Teacher remain for a whole year conversing with those who were awake?

"How can we believe even your statement that he appeared to you? How could he have appeared to you, when your opinions are opposed to his teaching? No, if you were visited and taught by him for a single hour and thus became an apostle, proclaim his utterances, interpret his teachings, love his apostles - and do not strive against me, who was his companion. For you have opposed me, the firm Rock, foundation of the church. If you were not an enemy, you would not slander me and disparage what is preached by me, as if I were obviously condemned and you were approved. If you call me condemned, you are accusing God who revealed the Christ to me, and are opposing the one who blessed me because of the revelation. Rather, if you really want to work together for the truth, first learn from us what we learned from him. Then, having become a disciple of the truth, become our fellow-worker.» (Homily XVII, 13–19)

Just substitute the name "Paul" for that of Simon in this dialogue, and you will recognize an early church dispute over apostolic credentials: Peter versus Paul. One the one side there is Paul: "I would have you know, brethren, that the gospel which was preached by me is not according to man. For I did not receive it from man, nor was I taught it, but it came through a revelation of Jesus Christ" (Gal. 1:11–12). On the other side stands Peter: "Blessed are you, Simon Bar-Jona! For flesh and blood has not revealed this to you, but my Father who is in heaven" (Matt. 16:17). Peter counts as an apostle because he heard the earthly Jesus in person: "One of the men who have accompanied us during all the time that the Lord Jesus went in and out among us, beginning from the baptism of John until the day when he was taken up from us—one of these men must become with us a witness to his resurrection" (Acts 1:21–22). To this, Paul's rejoinder: "Am I not an apostle? Have I not seen the Lord?" "Even if we have known Christ after the flesh, yet now we know him so no more" (2 Cor. 5:16). Peter is even made to refer to the earlier confrontation between Peter and *Paul* recorded in Galatians 2:11. It still rankled Peter that Paul had "opposed" and "condemned" him, words repeated from Galatians in the Clementine narrative.

Once Baur recognized Paul behind the mask of Simon here, the thought occurred to him that the same thing was going on in Acts 8:14–24.

Now when the apostles in Jerusalem heard that Samaria had received the word of God, they sent them Peter and John, who came down and prayed for them that they would receive the Holy Spirit. (For He had not yet fallen upon any of them; they had simply been baptized in the name of the Lord Jesus.) Then they began laying their hands on them, and they were receiving the Holy Spirit. Now when Simon saw that the Spirit was given through the laying on of the apostles' hands, he offered them money, saying, "Give this authority to me as well, so that everyone on whom I lay my hands may receive the Holy Spirit." But Peter said to him, "May your silver perish with you, because you thought you could acquire the gift of God with money! You have no part or share in this matter, for your heart is not right before God. Therefore, repent of this wickedness of yours, and pray to the Lord that, if possible, the intention of your heart will be forgiven you. For I see that you are in the gall of bitterness and in the bondage of unrighteousness." But Simon answered and said, "Pray to the Lord for me yourselves, so that nothing of what you have said may come upon me!"

Here's what Baur had to say about it.

What the apostle [Peter] affirmed that he was, the Magus wished to become. His proposal to the two apostles [Peter and John] was simply that they should bestow on him the apostolic office. He desired to have the power of commuting the Holy Ghost, in the same way as the apostles did so, according to the narrative of the Acts, where the communication of the Holy Ghost always follows on the laying on of the apostles' hands. . . . The facts out of which this charge [i.e., that] he was determined to be an apostle at any price arose must have been the two conferences which, according to the apostle's [i.e., Paul's] own narrative, he held with the older apostles at Jerusalem (Gal. i. 18, and ii. 1), as if his object in coming to Jerusalem had been to smuggle himself into the apostolic college. . . . The only occasion on which a question of money entered into his relations with the older apostles was when he was leaving them, and promised that he would do what he could for the support of the poor of Jerusalem in the Gentile Christian Churches in which he was to labour. . . . [His] opponents put the construction upon his efforts that his object was simply to purchase with this money the favour of the older apostles, and thus to attain at last what he had hitherto sought after in vain, his recognition as an apostle on the same level as the others.[292]

As we will soon see, his opponents may have been closer to the truth than Baur would allow.

Irenaeus informs us that Simon taught freedom from the Torah, which had been foisted upon humanity by wicked angels who had also created the world. Freed from the Law, we are instead saved by divine grace.

For since the angels ruled the world badly because each one of them coveted the principal power for himself, he had come to amend matters, and had descended, transfigured and assimilated to powers and principalities and angels, so that he might appear among men to be a man, while yet he was not a man. Thus, he was thought to have suffered in Judea, when he had not suffered. Moreover, the prophets uttered their predictions under the inspiration of those angels who formed the world; for which reason those who place their trust in him and [his companion] Helena no longer regard [the prophets], but, as being free, live as they please. For men are saved through his grace, and not on account of their own righteous actions. For such deeds are not righteous in the nature of things, but by mere accident, just as those angels who made the world, have thought fit to constitute them, seeking, by means of such precepts, to bring men into bondage. On this account, he pledged himself that the world should be dissolved, and that those who are his should be freed from the rule of them who made the world.

---

292. Ferdinand Christian Baur, *The Church History of the First Three Centuries.* Vol. I. Trans. Allan Menzies. Theological Translation Fund Library (London: Williams and Norgate, 1878), pp. 95–96. "But it was [Gustav] Volkmar who first completed the identification by recognizing in the magician's offer of money the apostle's subsidy from the western Churches" (p. 97).

All this sounds remarkably reminiscent of Paul! And that's no accident.

> "For by grace you have been saved through faith; and this is not your own doing, it is the gift of God—not because of works, lest any man should boast" (Ephesians 2:8–9). "Why then the law? It was added because of transgressions, till the offspring should come to whom the promise had been made; and it was ordained by angels through an intermediary. Now an intermediary implies more than one; but God is one" (Gal. 3:19–20). "Formerly, when you did not know God, you were in bondage to beings that by nature are no gods; but now that you have come to know God, or rather to be known by God, how can you turn back again to the weak and beggarly elemental spirits, whose slaves you want to be once more? You observe days, and months, and seasons, and years!" (Gal. 4:8–10). "And you, who were dead in trespasses and the uncircumcision of your flesh, God made alive together with him, having forgiven us all our trespasses, having canceled the bond which stood against us with its legal demands; this he set aside, nailing it to the cross. He disarmed the principalities and powers and made a public example of them, triumphing over them in him. Therefore let no one pass judgment on you in questions of food and drink or with regard to a festival or a new moon or a Sabbath" (Col. 2:13–16).

THE HISTORICAL SIMON

Eisenman indentifies the Magus with a magician named Simon of whom Josephus recounts that he helped Bernice convince her sister Drusilla to dump her husband King Azizus of Emesa, who had gotten circumcised in order to marry her, so she could take up with the uncircumcised Felix instead. Josephus' magician Simon is a Cypriot, while Acts' Simon Magus is said by later writers to hale from Gitta (ancient Gath, Goliath's home town) in Samaria, but this actually strengthens the connection, since it was natural to associate "Gitta" with the "Kittim," or Sea Peoples of Cyprus seeing that sea-board Philistia, including Gitta and Tyre, had long since become part of Samaria. It can be no coincidence that Acts associates Paul, too, with Felix, Drusilla, and Bernice (Acts 24:24–27; 25:13).

Morris Goldstein raises an intriguing possibility:

Another theory is that which takes [the Talmudic reference to the heretic] Ben Stada to refer to the pseudo-Messiah, Simon Magus, the magician mentioned in Acts 8:9–24. Further details are supplied by Justin Martyr, and in the Clementines which come from the Jewish-Christian-Gnostic group of the late second century. Simon Magus was born a Samaritan, went to Egypt as a young man and there acquired knowledge of magic. A former disciple of John the Baptist, he returned to Palestine with messianic pretentions, flourishing especially after the death of Dosthai [Dositheus], who had assumed leadership of the group left by John the Baptist. With the harlot Helene as his consort, Simon Magus proclaimed himself the Christ—*Stadios*—the Standing (Eternal) One. These facts and supplementary details in the *Recognitions* and *Homilies* bring about a close resemblance between Ben Stada, although, it must be noted, there is no record that [Simon] Magus was condemned and executed by the Jewish court at Lud [as was reported of Ben Stada]. There is, however, a striking similarity between the name Ben Stada and the self-designation of [Simon] Magus, Stadios. [Further,] it was suggested by H.P. Chajes and R.T. Herford that Ben Stada might be the Egyptian "false prophet" described by Josephus.[293]

Of course, this is the "prophet" who arrived in Jerusalem from Egypt and gathered a mob to come and watch him make the city walls of Jerusalem collapse, just as Joshua did when he "fit de battle of Jericho an' de walls come a' tumblin' down." Apprised of these

___

293. Goldstein, *Jesus in the Jewish Tradition*, pp. 61–62.

plans, the procurator Felix had his troops disperse the crowd, but in the confusion, the stymied prophet managed to escape, never to be heard from again. (Josephus, *Antiquities of the Jews* 20. 169–172; *Wars of the Jews* 2:261–263)

Or *was* he? Is it possible that Felix *did* apprehend him and instead of executing him, found him too fascinating a character to "waste"? Might he have decided to keep him around, as Herod Antipas had done with John the Baptist, visiting him often in prison to discuss theology (Mark 6:20)? Perhaps he decided that the prophet, with his wings clipped, might come in handy and added him to his retinue, which is just where we find Simon according to Josephus elsewhere. Remember, his association with this elite circle was an important clue for identifying Simon with Paul.

Lena Einhorn[294] argues that this unnamed (by Josephus) Egyptian was none other than our friend Paul. When the apostle is rescued from a seething mob, a Roman tribune asks him, "Are you not the Egyptian, then, who recently stirred up a revolt and led the four thousand men of the Assassins out into the wilderness?" (Acts 21:38). Paul answers, "I am a Jew, from Tarsus in Cilicia, a citizen of no mean city" (Acts 21:39). That's not a "no." No one says "the Egyptian" was a *native* of that country. Simon Magus wasn't. Ben Stada wasn't. Jeroboam wasn't. The Holy Family of Jesus wasn't.

Eisenman further notes that some manuscripts of Josephus name Felix's Simon "Atomus," which Eisenman connects with the Primal Adam doctrine he sees implied in Simon's claim to have been the Standing One (a divine title, implying "the Eternal, Unchanging One"), reincarnated many times. But there is a closer link still. Anyone can see that Luke has created the episode of Saul/Paul squaring off against Elymas the sorcerer (Acts 13:8 ff) as a Pauline counterpart

---

294. Lena Einhorn, *The Jesus Mystery: Astonishing Clues to the Identities of Jesus and Paul* (Lyons Press, 2007); Einhorn, *A Shift in Time: How Historical Documents Reveal the Surprising Truth about Jesus* (Yucca Publishing: 2016).

to Peter's contest with Simon Magus in Acts 8:9ff.

> So, being sent out by the Holy Spirit, they went down to Seleu-
> cia; and from there they sailed to Cyprus. When they arrived at
> Salamis, they proclaimed the word of God in the synagogues of
> the Jews. And they had John [John Mark, not the son of Zebedee]
> to assist them. When they had gone through the whole island as
> far as Paphos, they came upon a certain magician, a Jewish false
> prophet, named Bar-Jesus. He was with the proconsul, Sergius
> Paulus, a man of intelligence, who summoned Barnabas and Saul
> and sought to hear the word of God. But Elymas the magician (for
> that is the meaning of his name) withstood them, seeking to turn
> away the proconsul from the faith. But Saul, who is also called
> Paul, filled with the Holy Spirit, looked intently at him and said,
> "You son of the devil, you enemy of all righteousness, full of all
> deceit and villainy, will you not stop making crooked the straight
> paths of the Lord? And now, behold, the hand of the Lord is upon
> you, and you shall be blind and unable to see the sun for a time."
> Immediately mist and darkness fell upon him and he went about
> seeking people to lead him by the hand. Then the proconsul be-
> lieved, when he saw what had occurred, for he was astonished at
> the teaching of the Lord. (Acts 13:4–12; cf, 2 Macc. 3:27).

It is sort of a game of musical chairs. Bar-Jesus plays the same
Rasputin/Grima Wormtongue role Simon occupied vis-à-vis Festus,
Drusilla, Bernice and the gang. But he is also analogous to Saul of
Tarsus (i.e., Paul) in that he, too, is supernaturally struck blind on
account of his opposing the gospel message (cf, Acts 9:8–9). Sergius
Paulus is "Paul" as long as our Paul is "Saul," though Saul is revealed
to be "Paul" by the end of the story.[295]

---

295. Note that Paul is not said to have borne the Hebrew name of "Saul"
anywhere but in Acts, implying that it is but another function of Luke's catholicizing agenda: by adding this name Luke sought to tie Paul into the Old
Testament tradition in order to "de-Marcionize" the apostle. Hermann Detering, *The Falsified Paul: Early Christianity in the Twilight. Journal of Higher*

So Elymas is simply Simon Magus. And, what do you know? The Western Text of Acts gives the name as "Etoimas" or "Etomas" instead of Elymas! Thus, Simon Magus = Elymas = Etomas = Atomus = Josephus' Simon = Simon Magus. And "Atomus," which means "tiny one,"[296] is equivalent in meaning to "Paul," which means "little one."[297]

Elymas' patronymic "bar-Jesus" would seem to reflect the claim Simon made to have recently appeared in Judea as Jesus ("the Son"). Irenaeus records that Simon "taught that it was himself who appeared among the Jews as the Son, but descended in Samaria as the Father while he came to other nations in the character of the Holy Spirit." (And might this not mean that Simon claimed to be the Second Coming of Jesus?)

But wouldn't Jesus and Simon have been contemporaries? How could Simon have claimed he was "bar Jesus," the son of Jesus? Not a problem. Remember, Simon was supposed to be a docetic epiphany, descending from heaven in the form of an adult, just as Marcion understood Jesus to have done. The great Theosophist scholar G.R.S. Mead saw this. "For if he claimed to be a reincarnation of Jesus, appearing in Jerusalem as the Son, he could not have been contemporary with the apostles" . . . But this "supposition is not well-founded, and Simon was simply inculcating the esoteric doctrine of the various manifestations or descents [= avatars] of the one and the same Christ principle."[298]

We find, I think, another version of this Simonian claim in the Markan Passion narrative. Basilides noticed something odd in Mark 15:21–24: "And they compelled a passer-by, Simon of Cyrene, . . . to

---

Criticism. Vol. 10, no. 2 (Fall 2003), pp. 148, 166.

296. Just like Ray Palmer, the shrinking superhero "the Atom."

297. Detering, pp. 164–165.

298. G.R.S. Mead, *Simon Magus: An Essay on the Founder of Simonianism Based on the Ancient Sources with a Re-Evaluation of his Philosophy and Teachings* (1892; rpt. Chicago: Ares Publishers, 1979), p. 40.

carry his cross. And they brought him to the place called Golgotha
. . . and they crucified him." Hmmm . . . shouldn't the pronoun "him"
refer back to the last proper noun, which in this case is not "Jesus,"
but "Simon"?! So was Simon crucified in Jesus' stead? That sounds ri-
diculous until you remember that this actually was a current form of
docetism, akin to that found later in the Koran: "And because of their
saying: We slew the Messiah, Jesus son of Mary, Allah's messenger
- they slew him not nor crucified him, but it appeared so unto them;
and lo! those who disagree concerning it are in doubt thereof; they
have no knowledge thereof save pursuit of a conjecture; they slew
him not for certain" (4:157, Pickthall trans.). Irenaeus reports that

> He appeared on earth as a man and performed miracles. Thus he
> himself did not suffer. Rather, a certain Simon of Cyrene was com-
> pelled to carry his cross for him. It was he who was ignorantly
> and erroneously crucified, being transfigured by him, so that he
> might be thought to be Jesus. Moreover, Jesus assumed the form
> of Simon, and stood by laughing at them.

And Cyrene was another province of the Kittim, like Gitta, so we
have the identification made more sure.

HEAVEN AND HELEN

Irenaeus has more gossip to share:

> Having redeemed a certain woman named Helena from
> slavery at Tyre, a city of Phoenicia, he was in the habit of car-
> rying her about with him. He declared that this woman was
> the first conception of his mind, the mother of all, by whom,
> in the beginning, he conceived in his mind [the thought]
> of forming angels and archangels. For this Ennoia leaping
> forth from him, and comprehending the will of her father,

descended to the lower regions, and generated angels and powers, by whom also he declared this world was formed. But after she had produced them, she was detained by them through motives of jealousy, because they were unwilling to be looked upon as the progeny of any other being. As to himself, they had no knowledge of him whatever; but his Ennoia was detained by those powers and angels who had been produced by her. She suffered all kinds of insulting behavior from them, so that she could not return upwards to her father, but was even shut up in a human body, and for ages passed in succession from one female body to another, as from vessel to vessel. She was, for example, in that Helen on whose account the Trojan War was undertaken. . . .Thus she, passing from body to body, and suffering insults in every one of them, at last became a common prostitute; and she it was that was meant by the lost sheep [in Matt. 18:12–14?]. For this purpose, then, he had come that he might win her first, and free her from slavery, while he conferred salvation upon men, by making himself known to them.

This Helena also gets reincarnated within the New Testament, as we shall see, as she is hidden behind other names and characters. One of these is Queen Helena of Adiabene, a kingdom adjacent to Edessa, where her husband Abgarus (or Agbarus) reigned. At the behest of a Jewish missionary, Helena and her two sons converted to a sectarian form of Judaism. So enthusiastic was she in her new faith that she gave a large amount of money to buy grain to send to Jerusalem to relieve the famine in the time of Claudius Caesar. Paul is said to have brought such famine relief in Acts 11:27–30. He is probably to be understood here as Queen Helena's agent in her relief effort. And when the prophet Agabus predicts the famine, Luke has derived his name from that of Helena's husband Agbarus.[299]

---

299. Eisenman, pp. 878–882.

Simon/Paul and Helena lurk also in the story (or stories) of Mary Magdalene and Simon the leper. Simon the leper is Simon Magus. The description of the Antichrist in the Apocalypse of Elijah, seemingly intended as Simon Magus, describes him, hence Simon, as afflicted with leprosy.[300] Also, the underlying Aramaic word rendered "leper" is also reminiscent of "from Tyre,"[301] recalling how Simon rescued Helena from a brothel in Tyre. Well, the woman who anoints Jesus is undoubtedly Mary *Magdalene*, an epithet meaning "the hair-dresser," a euphemism in those days for the madam of a whore house.

WHO'S WHO?

Baur saw in Acts and the Homilies the creation of Simon Magus as a caricature of Paul (p. 93), but Hermann Detering goes farther, making Paul a sanitized version of the historical Simon, co-opted by the Catholic author of Acts. When Peter's opponent in the Homilies is named Simon, Detering argues, it is no fictive substitution for someone else, namely Paul. Quite the contrary: it *was* Simon Magus, not yet wearing his Pauline alias. In Acts 8:14–24 it's also Simon, though Luke, by using a character named Paul throughout Acts, means in chapter 8 to distinguish Paul from Simon in order to make "Paul" the upstanding Dr. Jekyll and Simon Magus the dastardly Mr. Hyde. "Paul," he makes a champion of "apostolic" (early catholic)[302] Christianity.

Acts' account of Paul's Damascus Road conversion is a blatant fiction based on Euripides' play *The Bacchae* as well as 2 Maccabees chapter 3.[303] But, as so often in Acts, its author has spun a congenial

300. Detering, pp. 167–168.

301. Detering, pp. 171–172.

302. Ernst Käsemann, *New Testament Questions of Today*. Trans. Wilfred F. Bunge (Philadelphia: Fortress Press, 1969), chapter XII, "Paul and Early Catholicism," pp. 236–251.

303. Robert M. Price, *The Amazing Colossal Apostle: The Search for the*

story to replace one that does not fit into the sanitized epic of Christian origins that he wants to promote. That story, so well hidden, does perhaps survive, just barely, in an omnibus of heresies penned by Epiphanius, fourth-century bishop of Salamis. He tells us that the Ebionites, the "Poor," descendants of the Jewish Christians of Jerusalem and environs,

> declare that he was a Greek [. . .] He went up to Jerusalem, they say, and when he had spent some time there, he was seized with a passion to marry the daughter of the priest. For this reason he became a proselyte and was circumcised. Then, when he failed to get the girl, he flew into a rage and wrote against circumcision and against the sabbath and the Law. (Epiphanius of Salamis, *Panarion* 30.16.6–9)

This business about Paul's spurned infatuations is standard fare in characterizations of "heretics" by their opponents, as a way of trivializing and discrediting their motives. But the notion that Paul had been a Gentile of some sort who converted to Judaism, then, wearying of the yoke of Torah, a burden to one not raised in that system of rules and mores, has the ring of plausibility. Of course, that formed the nucleus of the Pauline outreach to Gentiles: they need not bother adjusting to a host of regulations and taboos alien to their lifestyle and upbringing. To require Torah observance of Gentiles as a condition for baptism amounted to an unnecessary stumbling block in their path. And besides, is he not credited as saying "To the Jews I became as a Jew, in order to win Jews; to those under the law I became as one under the law—though not being myself under the law—in order to win those under the law" (1 Cor. 9:20).[304] That verse

---

Historical Paul (Salt Lake City: Signature Books, 2012), chapter 1,"The Legend of Paul's Conversion," pp.1–24.

304. I must admit I am tempted here to propose that Paul was referring to his (pretended) conversion to Judaism in order to "win" his damsel. But, don't worry, I won't.

invites a second look! The Ebionite claim puts a whole new light on it. Naturally, the Ebionite denial of Paul's Jewish pedigree sounds like a piece of polemic, as if to say, "They went out from us, but they were not of us; for if they had been of us, they would have continued with us; but they went out that they might be made manifest, that none of them were of us." But wouldn't it be better, if you wanted to vilify Paul, to call him an apostate Jew, period? What if the Ebionites knew what they were talking about? That would mean that "Paul" (Simon of Gitta) had converted not *from* Judaism, but rather *to* Judaism, albeit Jewish Torah "Christianity," that of the Qumran/Jerusalem Essenes. But he did not harbor there for long.

What would have been the real reason for his departure? I think we find the answer to that in the Dead Sea Scrolls. Eisenman points to the Habakkuk Pesher, where it tells of "the Spouter of Lying, who *led Many astray by building a worthless city on blood and erecting an Assembly on Lying.*"[305] The Spouter of Lies who "repudiated the Torah in the midst of the congregation" was our friend Paul. It was he who "founded a congregation on lies," namely the so-called "Simple Ones of Ephraim." These seem to have been converts from among the Gentile God-fearers who knew no better than to accept his preaching of freedom from the Torah.

The Pseudo-Clementines preserve a fascinating account of the sect of John the Baptist. The Baptizer, we learn, limited membership to thirty, perhaps suggesting allegiance to the old lunar calendar, one of the several features suggesting that John belonged to the Essene movement, as many have long suspected. When John was executed by Herod Antipas, a promising young fellow named Simon of Gitta was next in line to fill his sandals, but, as it happened, Simon was away in Egypt at the time, so another became the new leader, one Dositheus, a Samaritan like Simon. But Simon did eventually win out.

---

305. Eisenman, p. 259.

There was one John, a daily-baptist, who was also, according to the method of combination, the forerunner of our Lord Jesus; and as the Lord had twelve apostles, bearing the number of the twelve months of the sun, so also he [, John,] had thirty chief men, fulfilling the monthly reckoning of the moon, in which number was a certain woman called Helena, that not even this might be without a dispensational significance. For a woman, being half a man, made up the imperfect number of the triacontad; as also in the case of the moon, whose revolution does not make the complete course of the month. But of these thirty, the first and the most esteemed by John was Simon; and the reason of his not being chief after the death of John was as follows: He being absent in Egypt for the practice of magic, and John being killed, Dositheus[306] desiring the leadership, falsely gave out that Simon was dead, and succeeded to the seat. But Simon, returning not long after, and strenuously holding by the place as his own, when he met with Dositheus did not demand the place, knowing that a man who has attained power beyond his expectations cannot be removed from it. Wherefore with pretended friendship he gives himself for a while to the second place, under Dositheus. But taking his place after a few days among the thirty fellow-disciples, he began to malign Dositheus as not delivering the instructions correctly. And this he said that he did, not through unwillingness to deliver them correctly, but through ignorance. And on one occasion, Dositheus, perceiving that this artful accusation of Simon was dissipating the opinion of him with respect to many, so that they did not think that he was the Standing One, came in a rage to the usual place of meeting, and finding Simon, struck him with a staff. But it seemed to pass through the body of Simon as if he had been smoke. Thereupon Dositheus, being confounded, said to him, 'If you are the Standing One, I also will worship you.' Then Simon said that he was; and Dositheus, knowing that he himself was not the Standing One, fell

---

306. Stanley Jerome Isser, *The Dosithians: A Samaritan Sect in Late Antiquity*. Studies in Judaism in Late Antiquity Vol. 17 (Leiden: E.J. Brill, 1976), pp. 55–56.

down and worshipped; and associating himself with the twenty-nine chiefs, he raised Simon to his own place of repute; and thus, not many days after, Dositheus himself, while he (Simon) stood, fell down and died. (Homilies XXIII–XXIV)

I believe we have here another version of the clash between Simon/Paul/the Spouter of Lies and the Qumran/Essene/Ebionite community. Still another version meets us in Galatians 2:11–16:

But when Cephas came to Antioch I opposed him to his face, because he stood condemned. For before certain men came from James, he ate with the Gentiles; but when they came he drew back and separated himself, fearing the circumcision party. And with him the rest of the Jews acted insincerely, so that even Barnabas was carried away by their insincerity. But when I saw that they were not straightforward about the truth of the gospel, I said to Cephas before them all, "If you, though a Jew, live like a Gentile and not like a Jew, how can you compel the Gentiles to live like Jews?" We ourselves, who are Jews by birth and not Gentile sinners, yet who know that a man is not justified by works of the law but through faith in Jesus Christ, even we have believed in Christ Jesus, in order to be justified by faith in Christ, and not by works of the law, because by works of the law shall no one be justified.

Scholars have not failed to notice that Paul does not boast of having prevailed, as he surely would have had it gone in his favor. No, he just leaves Antioch in the hands of the "hypocrites" and moves on. In the same way, I have to suspect that the Homilies' account ending with Dositheus' dropping dead represents the same sort of masking as the pregnant silence about Paul's loss of face in Antioch, and that Dositheus actually just took his leave and set up sectarian shop down the street. *Or* it may well be that it *was* Simon who had to pack his bags and kick the dust of Qumran off his feet, as in the Galatians passage. At any rate, these bits and pieces seem to me all to mark the bitter separation of Paul/Simon from Jewish Christianity.[307]

REPROACH AND RAPPROCHEMENT

Baur took umbrage at the Lukan suggestion that Simon/Paul was trying to buy his way into the apostolic elite when he pledged himself to raise funds among his Gentile parishioners to subsidize the socialist collective in Jerusalem (and, I would add, Qumran).

> Then after fourteen years I went up again to Jerusalem with Barnabas, taking Titus along with me. I went up by revelation; and I laid before them (but privately before those who were of repute) the gospel which I preach among the Gentiles, lest somehow I should be running or had run in vain. But even Titus, who was with me, was not compelled to be circumcised, though he was a Greek. But because of false brethren secretly brought in, who slipped in to spy out our freedom which we have in Christ Jesus, that they might bring us into bondage—to them we did not yield submission even for a moment, that the truth of the gospel might be preserved for you. And from those who were reputed to be something (what they were makes no difference to me; God shows no partiality)— those, I say, who were of repute added nothing to me; but on the contrary, when they saw that I had been entrusted with the gospel to the uncircumcised, just as Peter had been entrusted with the gospel to the circumcised (for he who worked through Peter for the mission to the circumcised worked through me also for the Gentiles), and when they perceived the grace that was given to me, James and Cephas and John, who were reputed to be pillars, gave to me and Barnabas the right hand of fellowship, that we should

---

307. The whole mess is rather like the break between the mad zealot Aleister Crowley and the slightly less eccentric Order of the Golden Dawn, whereupon Crowley, "the Great Beast," formed his own sect, the Ordo Templi Orientis.

go to the Gentiles and they to the circumcised; only they would have us remember the poor, which very thing I was eager to do. (Gal. 2:1–10)

But I think there is some basis for the suspicion. Any way you look at it, it is hard not to understand "the Collection"[308] as tribute money (Rom. 15:25–27). And it is explicit in this passage that the money collection was a condition for the Pillars' imprimatur on Paul's efforts. The shrinking sect of the Poor was poor not only in spirit, but in cash flow as well. They must have looked with envy and amazement at the swelling ranks of Pauline Christianity. Rather than concluding he was doing something right and they were doing something wrong, they comforted themselves with the (no doubt sincere) thought that their rival was offering cheap grace by dropping the requirement of circumcision and Torah observance. Were the Paulinists seeking the esteem of men, not of God? Such watering down was abhorrent to the Poor and their Pillars—but maybe they could arrange for some of the Paulinist congregations' cash to find its way into worthier coffers! And there was a meeting of the minds. Simon will buy recognition by his former coreligionists, erasing the slight he had earlier suffered at their hands, exacting the proverbial revenge of success. And they will welcome a transference of earthly treasure.

But that was not all. Remember that Simon claimed a previous appearance among the Jews as the Son and went to the cross, though not actually suffering. To harvest funds from the numerous, thriving Paulinist franchises, the Pillars agreed not merely to authorize/recognize the Pauline mission (i.e., not to get in the way of his evangelism among Diaspora Jews); the only doctrinal demand he makes

---

308. Dieter Giorgi, *Remembering the Poor: The History of Paul's Collection for Jerusalem*. Trans. Ingrid Racz (Nashville: Abingdon Press, 1992); Keith F. Nickle, *The Collection: A Study in Paul's Strategy*. Studies in Biblical Theology No. 48 (London: SCM Press, 1966).

is to accept his celestial Christ, whose representative on earth he is. But they exact the right to fit this Christ into their own categories, making him a Jewish messiah. This entails historicizing "Jesus" by rewriting Old Testament tales.

Rivka Ulmer describes something like I have in mind: constructing a messianic saga by stitching together certain scripture passages.[309] She describes an ancient "gospel" of the yet-to-come Messiah Ephraim (Messiah ben Joseph), extending from a pre-Creation dialogue in which God asks the Messiah if he is willing to undergo terrible trials and pains in order to redeem Israel from their sins and defeat the pagans. He agrees. As he is experiencing these things, he finds he cannot endure them any longer and cries out to God. But he endures. The narrative is based on Psalm 22, Isaiah 53, Zechariah 12. Scholars debate whether it represents polemic against Christian messianic claims. But I wonder if instead we may see it as a spontaneous parallel analogous to the process whereby Mark created the Passion story.

The Qumran Twelve are retrojected into the resultant Jesus story, along with the three Pillars, James, John, and Cephas/Peter as the inner circle. The Twelve as Jesus' itinerant lieutenants are blatantly anachronistic, as during the (fictive) ministry Jesus would not have had a community for them to head up.[310] The triumvirate of the Pillars appear,[311] distinguished from the rest, for no stated reason, with

---

309. Rivka Ulmer, "Psalm 22 in Pesiqta Rabbati: The Suffering of the Jewish Messiah and Jesus" in Zev Garber, ed., *The Jewish Jesus: Revelation, Reflection, Reclamation.* Shofar Supplements in Jewish Studies (West Lafayette, IN: Purdue University Press, 2011), pp. 106–128.

310. Walter Schmithals, *The Office of Apostle in the Early Church.* Trans. John E. Steely (Nashville: Abingdon Press, 1969), pp. 67–87, argued that though the historical Jesus did have disciples, they did not include an elite group of twelve. That body, he suggested, was subsequently constituted as such because of a joint resurrection appearance.

311. But do they match? Is "James" supposed to be James, the same-named Pillar? Roman Catholics believe they are the same because James the "brother" of Jesus was James, son of Zebedee.

Jesus at the Transfiguration. The story is intended to allow them to have a vision of Simon/Paul's celestial Christ, thus placing them on a level with Paul. They also witness the raising of Jairus' daughter and are the privileged recipients of the Olivet Discourse. They owe their anachronistic and arbitrary (i.e., unexplained) presence on such occasions to their original role as the Pillars of the Ebionite/Essene community.

The alliance does not last: the Pillars send agents to dog Paul's heels, as we see in Galatians 1:6–10; 2:11–12; 3:1–5; 4:8–11, 15–21; 5:1–4, 9–12; 6:12–13. If they can get his converts to switch sides in great numbers, they will not need the heretic! They can exact tribute/offerings directly!

Is this in fact the way it happened? Who knows? But my proposal might be seen to solve certain long-standing problems and to make sense of some odd bits of evidence we have not known what to do with and have ignored. Thomas Kuhn suggests that, in order to field a new paradigm, we must begin with the "anomalous data" left over by the previous paradigm.[312] What if, up till now, we have been putting the cart before the horse? Or even leaving the horse in the barn!

---

312. "Discovery commences with the awareness of anomaly." Kuhn, p. 52.

CONCLUSION

My hypothesis is that the widespread position that Jesus must be assumed to have been essentially a devout practitioner of Second Temple Judaism is the product of ecumenical and apologetical agendas and does not survive close, genuinely critical scrutiny. *Judaizing Jesus* bucks an overwhelming theological-ecumenical trend, challenging the prevalent consensus of the scholarly mainstream precisely by employing the accepted tools of critical exegesis. My goal has been to demonstrate the extent to which the consensus is actually theology masquerading as historical description. Scholars today are readily willing to call the bluff of traditional conservative biblical scholarship without noticing they may be guilty of the same kind of wishful thinking. Even to raise this question is controversial in the present climate, but to do so is the only way, not only to test the Jewish Jesus hypothesis, but also to maintain any scholarly integrity, even as Albert Schweitzer famously did. We have no hope of identifying the Jesus of history as long as we are unwilling to discover a Jesus who may defy and disappoint our cherished assumptions. What if today's ecumenically-minded Jesus scholars are merely repeating what the Christian Torah sect did: artificially Judaizing the Jesus figure from a wholly different world of belief?

THY NIEBUHR AS THYSELF

My complaint in this book has been that the desire for Jewish-Christian dialogue has turned instead into *negotiation*, the goal apparently being to forge a paper compromise, a peace treaty that will bring about a cessation of theological (and real-world) hostilities. This is a big mistake. First, it results in a tiny elite of ecumenical diplomats who have only alienated the religious constituencies they think they represent. Second, it tempts ecumenically-minded biblical scholars to falsify the gospel data to create a "usable" Jesus. As an alternative, I have tried to demonstrate there are other viable historical models for Jesus, some familiar, others arising from neglected data. It's not Rabbi Jesus or nothing. Besides, the whole endeavor is not only totally unnecessary but wrong-headed from the start. Here are a few thoughts toward a better approach.

H. Richard Niebuhr posited a theology of "confession," confessing one's own faith without an accompanying denial of other faiths. One might and should stick to rejoicing in one's own faith without sticking one's pious nose into other people's religious business. Must my creed include the criticism or denial of yours?

> A critical historical theology . . . may try to develop a method not applicable to all religions but to the particular faith to which its historical point of view is relevant. Such theology in the Christian church cannot, it is evident, be an offensive or defensive enterprise which undertakes to prove the superiority of the Christian faith to all other faiths; but it can be a confessional theology which carries on the work of self-criticism and self-knowledge in the church.[313]
>
> Relativism does not imply subjectivism and skepticism. It is not evident that the man who is forced to confess that his view of

---

313. H. Richard Niebuhr, *The Meaning of Revelation* (New York: Macmillan, 1960), p. 13.

things is conditioned by the standpoint he occupies must doubt the reality of what he sees. It is not apparent that one who knows his concepts are not universal must also doubt that they are concepts of the universal, or that one who understands how all his experience is historically mediated must believe that nothing is mediated through history.[314]

We are enabled to see why we can speak of revelation only in connection with our own history without either affirming or denying its reality in the histories of other communities into whose inner life we cannot penetrate without abandoning ourselves and our community.[315]

Thomas J.J. Altizer was, as I read him, operating within a similar conceptual framework when it came to Judaism.

We were speaking in the context of Judaism. I think a Jew can indeed know a transcendent God. The Jew lives in a kind of eternal covenant with God, and he can preserve this because he lives in exile—because he is not totally involved in our history [in which the transcendent God has died]. . . . The Jew actually is in communion with that ancient epiphany of God—has preserved and perpetuated that moment in faith. . . . It's a false God as far as the Christian is concerned. But I see no reason for the Christian to attack it as such.[316]

Paul Tillich has somewhat the same idea, I think, but states it from the Christian end of the telescope:

In faith it is certain that for historical mankind in its unique, con-

---

314. Niebuhr, ibid.

315. Niebuhr, p. 60.

316. Thomas J.J. Altizer as interviewed by William Braden. In Braden, *The Private Sea: LSD and the Search for God* (New York: Bantam Books, 1968), p. 140.

tinuous development, as experienced here and now, Christ is the center. But faith cannot judge about the future destiny of historical mankind and the way it will come to an end. Jesus is the Christ for us, namely, for those who participate in the historical continuum which he determines in its meaning.[317]

I admit, it sounds kind of tautological, as if to say, "For those who define history by Jesus Christ, Jesus is the definition of history." Yeah? So? But there is a point here, and it is much like that of H. Richard Niebuhr. The "world" of Christian existence is self-referential and self-contained, a Leibnizian monad co-existent with others adjacent to it, but not interpenetrating with them. Insofar as "Jews" and "Judaism" figure in the Christian monad, they are functions of Christianity and have nothing to do with Jews and Judaism as they exist in the Jewish monad. This is why the Christian, on Niebuhr's understanding, can confess his faith in Jesus as the savior of the world, yet without actually condemning or criticizing Jews or the Jewish faith. Their theological indifference to Jesus as Savior and Messiah is simply irrelevant to Christianity (and vice versa).

It's like when Wittgenstein illustrated the nature of "language games" by positing a scenario in which an apocalyptic believer asks, "Wittgenstein, do you think the Second Coming of Christ is at hand?" The philosopher would find himself stumped. If he was a player in the other's language game, his answer of "no" would mean "not now; maybe later." But he is an outsider, so his negative reply would mean, "Sorry, but I just don't see things in those terms."[318] He's not located in that monad. Likewise, when a Christian affirms Jesus as the Messiah, he does not, need not, impinge upon the Jew's belief

---

317. Paul Tillich, *Systematic Theology: Volume II, Existence and the Christ* (Chicago: University of Chicago Press, 1957), p. 101.

318 Ludwig Wittgenstein, *Lectures & Conversations on Aesthetics, Psychology and Religious Belief*, ed., Cyril Barrett (Berkeley: University of California Press, n.d.), This is my paraphrased summation of a portion of the argument on pp.53 ff.

that Messiah has not yet appeared—or the Islamic belief that Jesus is not God's Son. Different monads. Different language games.

Nor is this some new-fangled theological gimmick. It is as old as the Buddhist, Jainist, Sufi parable of the Blind Men and the Elephant. Here is John Godfrey Saxe's version.

THE BLIND MEN AND THE ELEPHANT.
A **HINDOO** FABLE.

I.

T'was six men of Indostan
To learning much inclined,
Who went to see the Elephant
(Though all of them were blind),
That each by observation
Might satisfy his mind.

II.

The *First* approached the Elephant,
And happening to fall
Against his broad and sturdy side,
At once began to bawl:
"God bless me!—but the Elephant
Is very like a wall!"

III.

The *Second*, feeling of the tusk,
Cried: "Ho!—what have we here
So very round and smooth and sharp?
To me 't is mighty clear
This wonder of an Elephant
Is very like a spear!"

IV.

The *Third* approached the animal,
And happening to take
The squirming trunk within his hands,
Thus boldly up and spake:
"I see," quoth he, "the Elephant
Is very like a snake!"

V.

The *Fourth* reached out his eager hand,
And felt about the knee.
"What most this wondrous beast is like
Is mighty plain," quoth he;
"'T is clear enough the Elephant
Is very like a tree!"

VI.

The *Fifth*, who chanced to touch the ear,
Said: "E'en the blindest man
Can tell what this resembles most;
Deny the fact who can,
This marvel of an Elephant
Is very like a fan!"

VII.

The *Sixth* no sooner had begun
About the beast to grope,
Than, seizing on the swinging tail
That fell within his scope,
"I see," quoth he, "the Elephant
Is very like a rope!"

VIII.

And so these men of Indostan
Disputed loud and long,
Each in his own opinion
Exceeding stiff and strong,
Though each was partly in the right,
And all were in the wrong!
So, oft in theologic wars
The disputants, I ween,
Rail on in utter ignorance
Of what each other mean,
And prate about an Elephant
Not one of them has seen!

Saxe takes the analogy in a skeptical direction, a well-founded one as it seems to me, but I see in it, as I think the Buddhists, Jainists, and Sufis did, a vision of the Deity transcending all the metaphors, concepts, and doctrines we employ to try to grasp it. "Such knowledge is too wonderful for me; it is high; I cannot attain to it" (Psalm 40:5). And thus it will always be premature for us to declare an irreconcilable contradiction between the doctrines of different religions. Who knows if farther up, further out, the parallel lines may meet? In case you hadn't noticed, Christians already take this approach to the Trinity. The seeming incompatibility of the One and the Three, they say, is no contradiction but rather a Holy Mystery. Every attempt to explain and define it is premature and inevitably produces heresies. Why might the differences between the religions not be deemed a Holy Mystery, too?

And do we really even need "dialogue"? Mutual understanding, sure. But, again, I believe the best course was set long ago by Gotthold Lessing in his reworking of a story from Boccaccio's *Decameron* that appears in the former's play *Nathan the Wise*. In it the Muslim

Saladin asks the Jewish sage Nathan (a thinly veiled Maimonides) which religion is the true faith: Judaism, Christianity, or Islam? Here is a handy summary.

> An ancient Oriental possessed a priceless ring which had the power to render its wearer beloved by God and man. He passed it on by will to his favourite son, with instructions that he should do likewise. So it passed down many generations until it came to one who had three sons all equally dear to him. Not wishing to favour one more than the others, he had two replicas made, and thus gave each of his sons a ring. After his death each son claimed to possess the true ring, and a quarrel broke out between them. The true ring could not be identified—"almost as for us the true faith is now beyond discovery." A judge brought in to arbitrate decided that none of the three quarreling brothers could rightly claim to possess it. Presumably the true ring must therefore have been lost, and the father must have had three rings made to replace it. Nevertheless, by love and brotherly conduct each should try to show that his own ring possessed the power of the ancient ring. Only so, if at all, might the identity of the true ring be determined.[319]

Why not make it a friendly competition in which everyone may win? Then it may not matter which one is the "true" faith, if not in fact all three? And you can see such a program in action at any local Clergy Association meeting. There you will find nothing but cooperation in humanitarian service, with divisive doctrines left at the door. It's a winning formula. Cooperation, not compromise. I believe the slogan is "Doctrine divides; service unites." Precisely! And it does not mean doctrines are unimportant in themselves. They do have a properly regulatory function within any particular religion. It's just that, for some purposes they tend to get in the way.

---

319. Henry Chadwick's summary in his "Introduction" to Chadwick, ed. and trans., *Lessing's Theological Writings*. A Library of Modern Religious Thought (Stanford: Stanford University Press, 1957), p. 27.

So if we find that modern scholars have done to Jesus what Matthew did to Mark, we need not mourn the loss of the ecumenically handy "Rabbi Jesus." He has, like the Golem of Prague, reverted to the clay from which he was made.

ABOUT THE AUTHOR

Robert M. Price is the host of the podcasts The Bible Geek and The Human Bible, as well as the author of many books. He is the founder and editor of the *Journal of Higher Criticism*.